Royal Monastic

Princess Ileana of Romania

by Bev. Cooke

CONCILIAR PRESS MINISTRIES † BEN LOMOND, CALIFORNIA

Royal Monastic: Princess Ileana of Romania
Copyright © 2008 Bev. Cooke

Published by   Conciliar Press Ministries
                   P.O. Box 76
                   Ben Lomond, CA 95005-0076

All Old Testament quotations, unless otherwise identified, are from the
Orthodox Study Bible, © 2008 by St. Athanasius Academy of Orthodox Theology
(published by Thomas Nelson, Inc., Nashville, Tennessee) and are used by permission. New Testament quotations are from the New King James Version of the
Bible, © 1982 by Thomas Nelson, Inc., and are used by permission.

Printed in the United States of America

ISBN 10: 1-888212-32-2
ISBN 13: 978-1-888212-32-7

Cover and interior designed by Katherine Hyde

Cover photo: Curtea de Arges Monastery, Romania
Photo copyright © Ciprian-Florin Dumitrescu (shutterstock.com)

Interior photos courtesy of the Orthodox Monastery of the Transfiguration,
unless otherwise noted.

For none of us lives to himself, and no one dies to himself. For if we live, we live to the Lord; and if we die, we die to the Lord. Therefore, whether we live or die, we are the Lord's.
—Romans 14:7–8

To Matushka Donna Farley and to Mavis Andrews:
My sisters of the heart.

Acknowledgments

Always to my family. I treasure them and wouldn't know what to do without them. For this project, Al and Mark provided information about the world wars, military definitions and explanations—thank you guys! I love you all!

To Joe Cummings—for more battles of the world wars, political implications of war, and that great book with the maps of the war. And for all the coffee and conversations at Tim Horton's.

To Dara Lehner for the photographs, friendship, phone calls, and general support, including a ten-hour trip across two states just to visit me. You are a gem, a wonder and a blessing, Dara.

To Valerie Motet and Mira Davidson for their support and encouragement. Valerie told me about Romania and Castle Bran and HM King Michael. She and her daughter, Mira, translated letters for me and prayed for me through this entire journey. Thank you so much for your generosity and kindness.

To all of my other Romanian friends—Monalisa and Kostel, Gabriella, and the entire Surdu families especially, who showed me how generous and warm-hearted Romanians are, and how tenaciously they've clung to their faith in the face of unrelenting oppression and persecution.

A thank-you will never be enough for the monastics of the Orthodox Monastery of the Transfiguration. They helped with research materials, their time, their support, prayers, and their memories of Mother Alexandra. They showed me the love of Christ in day-to-day living.

Thank you to Tom Kinter and the Rev. Terry Elsberry. Tom's web pages on Princess Ileana provided information. Father Terry graciously answered my questions about Ileana and Queen Marie. His book on Queen Marie deeply informed my work. Thank you so much for your time, Father Terry!

A major thank-you to the staff at Conciliar Press—Jane, Katherine, Carla, Shelly, and Heather. It was Conciliar's suggestion I take on this project, and I owe them a huge debt for the privilege and wonder of having "met" the extraordinary woman who is Mother Alexandra.

To Mother herself, for her prayers and intercessions. A number of minor miracles accompanied this journey, which leaves me even more in awe of God and His mercy and love. And thank you to the Lord, without whom I could do nothing.

Contents

Section I

A Tumultuous Childhood

TIMELINE 1900–1918

YEAR	COUNTRY	EVENT
1900	Romania	Princess Marie (Mignon), daughter of Ferdinand and Marie, born
	Britain	Death of Ileana's grandfather, Prince Alfred, Duke of Saxe-Coburg and Gotha, son of Queen Victoria
1901	USA	Assassination of President McKinley
	Britain	Ileana's great-grandmother, Queen Victoria, dies
1903	Romania	Prince Nicolas (Nicky) born
	USA	First powered, heavier-than-air manned flight—the Wright Brothers
1904	USA	Theodore Roosevelt elected president
1906	Britain	HMS Dreadnought commissioned, revolutionizing naval ship design & sparking a naval arms race
1907	Romania	Peasants revolt over land ownership
	Britain	Scouting movement begins
1908	Britain	Boy Scouts formed
	Britain	Suffragettes storm House of Commons
1909	Romania	Princess Ileana born
	USA	William Howard Taft elected president
	Britain	Girl Guides formed
1910	Canada	Royal Canadian Navy founded
	Britain	King Edward VII dies; succeeded by George V
1911	Canada	Robert Borden becomes prime minister
1913	Romania	Prince Mircea born
	USA	Woodrow Wilson becomes president
1914	Sarajevo	Archduke Ferdinand of Austria-Hungary assassinated
	Europe	World War I begins
	Romania	Declares neutrality in war; King Carol I dies, succeeded by Ferdinand (Ileana's father)
1915	France	Battle of Ypres—poison gas used for the first time
1916	Romania	Romania declares for Allies; Germans advance to Brasov; Mircea dies; evacuation to Jassy; fall of Bucharest
	France	Battle of the Somme—first use of tanks in war

YEAR	COUNTRY	EVENT
1917	Britain/ Middle East	Gaza, Jerusalem taken from Ottoman Empire
	USA/Europe	USA enters WWI
	France	Battle of Vimy Ridge
	Russia	October Revolution—Bolsheviks come to power; armistice with Germany
1918	World	Influenza pandemic worldwide—killed as many as 40–100 million
	Romania	Armistice with Germany. All Allies leave Romania
	France	Second Battle of the Marne
	Russia	Assassination of royal family
	Europe	Germany surrenders—end of war

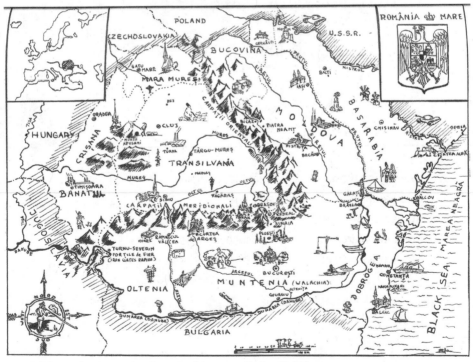

Map of Romania drawn by Ileana's oldest son, Stefan Habsburg

Ileana's Romania

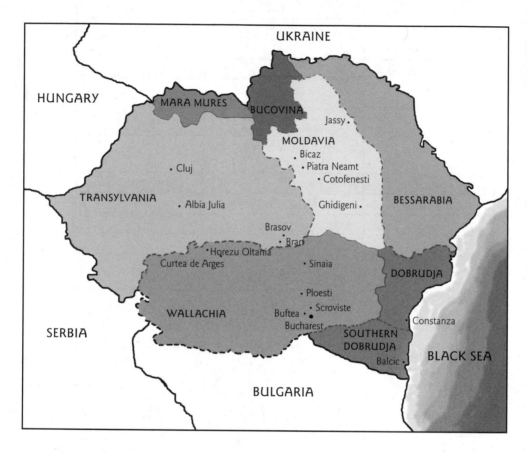

International boundaries: Solid black lines
Internal boundaries: Solid gray lines
Romania 1861–1919: Dotted borders
Romania Mare 1919–1940: All shaded areas
Modern Romania: All except Bessarabia and Southern Dobrudja

CHAPTER ONE

Birth & Family

Let everything that breathes praise the Lord. (Psalm 150:6)

Imagine This

It is January 5, 1909. The snowy streets of Bucharest, on the plains of Wallachia in Romania, bustle as people go about their business. Men stride along the streets, avoiding the horse-drawn carriages as they move to meetings and offices, and unload wagons at warehouses. A few motorcars driven by the rich putter around the horses and carriages. Women hurry to shops wrapped in their shawls and coats to avoid the cold winter wind that blows the snow around their fashionable skirt hems as they step from their carriages. Peasants, dressed in warm woolen *gluges*, or cloaks, move along the streets. Steam billows out of the bakeries and grocer's shops as customers enter and leave, enveloping passersby in the scent of freshly baked bread, cinnamon and nutmeg.

The cold, clear air is shattered by a cannon blast. Another one breaks the sudden silence, and instead of panicking, people in the streets begin to cheer. The roads and alleyways crowd with people as they pour out of the buildings to hear and count the cannon blasts that boom and echo through the city.

"Twenty-one!" exclaims one man, turning to his friend. His breath steams in the cold air, and they shiver without their coats, but for the

13

moment, they scarcely notice. "Another princess for Romania!" His friend nods, claps him on the back, and the two duck into a coffee shop to toast the safe arrival of Princess Ileana.

On the outskirts of the city in Cotroceni* Palace, Crown Princess Marie, "with the new little world wanderer pressed to my heart," listens to the royal salute in "deep, conscious, almost sacred emotion."

Mother and daughter are wrapped in their own safe world, concerned only for each other.

In an hour, Crown Prince Ferdinand will arrive to formally acknowledge this child as his, and therefore a princess of Romania. But for now, the baby has been bathed and wrapped and is cuddled in her mother's arms and love, as she always will be. Born with enormous dark blue eyes, she has already captivated her mother and is well on her way to becoming Princess Marie's "child of my soul."

Born on Romanian soil, baptized and raised in the Orthodox Church, a member of the royal family of a land that had only recently found its nationality, Princess Ileana came from the most powerful families in the world.

Princess Ileana with her mother, Queen Marie

* Words marked with * are explained in the Glossary beginning on page 190.

Her mother, Crown Princess Marie of Romania, was the granddaughter of both Queen Victoria of Britain and Tsar* Alexander II of Russia. Crown Prince Ferdinand, Ileana's father, was the son of Prince Leopold of Hohenzollern (in what is now Germany) and the Infanta* Antonia of Portugal. He was the nephew of Prince Karl Eitel Friedrich, also known as King Carol of Romania.

There were no Romanians in Ileana's ancestry. The country had not been conquered by Britain or Germany, so how did a German princeling and the quintessential British princess give birth to a Romanian citizen, a princess, the daughter of the heirs to that country's throne?

Romania has been a nation and a people since before the Roman Empire, but for most of her history, her land has been overrun by invaders. In a period of only one hundred years, from 1754 to 1854, the Russians and Turks invaded Romania no less than six times each.

Finally, in 1856, the Romanians, tired of being overrun and conquered, formed two small nations: Wallachia and Moldavia. Each area was governed by a prince elected by the parliament. In a brilliant move in 1861, both parliaments elected the same man, Alexander Cuza, to be their prince, and effectively became one country. Unfortunately, Romanians, excited about the possibilities of a single country, couldn't agree about how to run the new nation, and Alexander was forced to abdicate after only a year.

One man had an idea that worked. Ion Bratianu thought that to really unite Romania, they needed a foreign prince, one who wasn't related by either birth or marriage to the rest of the government. That way, he would be above the contentions every government has to endure.

In order to keep the king and his family from the internal political divisions, Romania's constitution forbade the heirs to the throne to marry a Romanian. In addition, it specified that the children of the royal family be raised as Orthodox Christians.

So on May 22, 1866, Prince Karl Eitel—Ileana's great-uncle—stepped off the train in Bucharest, took his oath of office, and became Prince Carol of Romania. After he had proved to himself and to Romania that he could rule, he was crowned king in 1899.

He and his wife, Queen Elizabeth (also known as Carmen Sylva, a renowned author and artist) had no heir, so he appointed his nephew

Ferdinand, Ileana's father, as crown prince to the throne of Romania.

Prince Ferdinand and Princess Marie were married in January of 1893. Their honeymoon was the train ride from Germany to Bucharest, and they moved into the royal palace in the center of the city. Shortly afterward, Marie declared the place too dark and gloomy, and she and Prince Ferdinand took over the abandoned monastery of Cotroceni on the outskirts of Bucharest. She remodeled and redecorated the monastery into a warm, welcoming palace that felt like home.

Their first son, Carol, was born in October of 1893, and the family grew with the additions of Elisabeta or Lisabeta in October of 1894, and Marie, or Mignon, as the family called her, in January of 1900. Nicolas ("Nicky"), the second son, was born in August of 1903. Ileana joined the family in 1909.

Prince Carol, especially, was captivated by the newest addition. He spent hours reading to Ileana, and as she grew, playing with her. They had a favorite game in which Carol, in spite of being sixteen years older than his sister, would put the little girl on his train set and give her rides on it. She would squeal with glee and lean, breathless with terrified delight, into the turns. She'd make herself as tiny as she could to fit through the tunnels, but by the time she was three or four it was a tight fit, and in later years she remembered being squeezed as the train rocketed through the painted plaster caves.

But by 1913, when Ileana was four and Prince Carol was twenty, he was growing away from her. In spite of their love, his royal duties and more adult interests took him away from his four-year-old sister.

However much Ileana may have missed Carol's attention, the void was filled when, on January 3, her brother Mircea was born. "Ileana loved him with motherly ardor and Mircea adored Ileana more than anyone on this earth; more than his mother, more than his nurse," Queen Marie said of them. Ileana herself called him "the great love of my heart."

Ileana's happy, contented nature overlaid a deep and earnest outlook on life. She seemed able from the earliest ages to relate to people on an almost instinctive level. Her mother was devoutly religious and passed on her faith to her daughter. Ileana loved the monasteries she visited with her mother and reveled in the incense, candles, and holy atmosphere of the liturgies she attended. Her first home was the converted monastery of

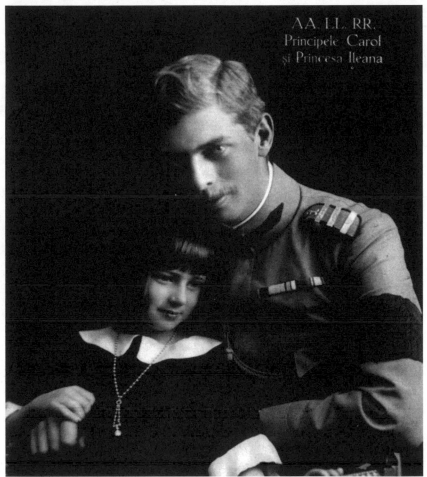

AA. LL. RR.
Principele Carol
și Princesa Ileana

Princess Ileana with her oldest brother, Prince Carol

Cotroceni, and there she was surrounded from her birth by the accumulated peace and piety that centuries of prayer and contemplation bestow on such a place. She always had an abiding interest in God and the angels, which was deepened late one night.

❧❧❧ Ileana Remembers ❧❧❧

It was early morning, when I was seven years old, that I saw the angels. I am as sure of it now as I was then. I was not dreaming, nor 'seeing things'—I just know they were there, plainly, clearly, distinctly. I was neither astonished nor afraid. I was not even awed—I was only terribly pleased. I wanted to talk to them and touch them.

Our night nursery was lit by the dawn and I saw a group of angels standing, as if chatting, around my brother's bed. I was aware of this, although I could not hear their voices. They wore long flowing gowns of various soft-shaded colors. Their hair came to their shoulders, and differed in color from fair and reddish to dark brown. They had no wings. At the foot of my brother Mircea's bed stood one heavenly being, a little aside from the others—taller he was, and extraordinarily beautiful, with great white wings. In his right hand he carried a lighted taper; he did not seem to belong to the group of angels gathered around the bed. He clearly stood apart and on watch. I knew him to be the guardian angel. I then became aware that at the foot of my own bed stood a similar celestial creature. He was tall, his robe was dark blue with wide, loose sleeves. His hair was auburn, his face oval, and his beauty such as I cannot describe because it was comparable to nothing human. His wings swept high and out behind him. One hand was lifted to his breast, while in the other he carried a lighted taper. His smile can only be described as angelic; love, kindness, understanding, and assurance flowed from him. Delighted, I crawled from under the bedcovers and, kneeling up against the end of the bed, I stretched out my hand with the ardent wish to touch my smiling guardian, but he took a step back, put out a warning hand, and gently shook his head. I was so close to him I could have reached him easily. "Oh, please don't go," I cried; at which words all the other angels looked toward me, and it seemed I heard a silvery laugh, but of this sound I am not so certain, though I know they laughed. Then they vanished.

In spite of Princess Ileana's awe, the experience of seeing the angels faded into the background of her mind, as events in the outer world claimed her own and her family's attention. The visit from the angels was the last truly peaceful experience she would have for the next few years. As she herself said, "My childhood had been peaceful, but in a way I remember it now only as a far-off dream of a story I was once told."

CHAPTER TWO

Heartbreak & War

All these are the beginning of sorrows. (Matthew 24:8)

hough Ileana and her brothers and sisters grew up safe and priv-
ileged, there were some things from which they could not be
protected, no matter how vigilant their parents, no matter how
royal their blood.

While Ileana and the rest of the family enjoyed a summer picnic with
their Russian cousins in 1914, most of the rest of Europe was exploding.

In July, the crown prince of the Austro-Hungarian Empire, Archduke
Franz Ferdinand, and his wife, Sophie Cochek, were assassinated by a
Serbian revolutionary in the town of Sarajevo in Bosnia. Austria declared
war, and with the complicated treaties and alliances that existed in Europe
at the time, the entire continent was embroiled within weeks.

Tension in Romania was great, and nowhere more so than in Ileana's
family. King Carol and Queen Elizabeth were German and naturally sided
with Austria-Hungary and the German alliance. But Ileana's mother was
staunchly British and equally certain that Romania should support Britain.
Tensions at the family dinner table rose as Queen Elizabeth tried to convince Princess Marie that Romania's only hope lay with the Germans.
"Darling Missy," Queen Elizabeth said to Princess Marie on one occasion, "Germans must become lords of the world for the good of human-
ity. Besides, my dear Missy, England has to fall—her women have become

Visit with the family of Tsar Nicholas II of Russia, 1914. Ileana is at center on the lap of Grand Duchess Tatiana.

immoral!" It was here, perhaps, that Ileana began to learn the art of diplomacy, for as passionately British as her mother was, she bit her tongue and refused to answer her aunt-in-law's taunts.

On August 3, 1914, the Romanian government voted to remain neutral. But the tension of balancing the disputed positions continued to run through the family and the nation, weakening King Carol's already frail health. In October of 1914, he died, and Ileana's father, Ferdinand, became king.

Ferdinand maintained the tenuous neutrality for two years, until 1916, when it seemed that Ileana's entire world was crumbling. First, in early August, her great-aunt Queen Elizabeth died. She was buried at Curtea de Arges, beside her husband.

On August 27, King Ferdinand signed the declaration of war against the Central Powers* and entered the war on the British side. By early September, the Germans were bombing Bucharest, and it wasn't long before the Germans targeted Cotroceni and the royal family. By God's grace, by the time the bombs made a direct hit on the gardens of Ileana's home, the family had moved to Buftea, the residence of one of Queen Marie's closest advisors and a great friend of Ileana's, Prince Barbu Stirbey.* Ileana called him "the Good Man."

Things grew grimmer as the Germans and their allies, the Serbians, advanced relentlessly. Both Queen Marie and King Ferdinand believed royalty were the "first servants of the state," and they were determined that their children should learn to shoulder their share of the duty. So Queen Marie and her daughters visited the hospitals filled with wounded and dying soldiers, bringing cigarettes, conversation, meals, and a bit of good cheer.

Queen Marie recorded in her diary on the sixth of October, 1916, that "Ileana came for the first time to the hospital, and helped serve meals to the wounded with a little white cloth on her head like those I wear."

ᕼᕼᕼ ᕼᕼᕼ ᕼᕼᕼ Imagine This ᕼᕼᕼ ᕼᕼᕼ ᕼᕼᕼ

There's a long, dark room. High on the wall, windows let in bright sunlight, which falls in squares on the white tiled floor but doesn't seem to relieve the gloom. Beds run down the length of the room, too many to count—one every few feet. Men in the beds talk, groan, cry out. The smell is of disinfectant, but underneath there is an odor of rot. It's the smell of infection underneath the cutting sharpness of the bleach.

The door in the far wall opens, and the smell of cooked food permeates the space, bringing a stir from the men. Women in white, pushing massive trolleys full of laden plates, glasses, and cups, move swiftly down the center aisle between the beds. Behind them move a few men in army uniforms, highly polished black boots clicking on the linoleum. A stir begins near the doors, and all eyes turn to the last nurse—the one with the soldiers, the one with a small girl by her side.

The woman wears a white nursing uniform. Her skirt reaches to the top of her white ankle boots, and the starched white apron sports a garden of medals and crosses. The white nursing wimple frames a beautiful, kind face creased in a warm, motherly smile.

The child by her side is clearly her daughter—they share the same shape of face, the same flawless complexion, and the same attitude of concern. The young girl wears a white dress and a white handkerchief pinned to her chin-length dark hair, in imitation of her mother's nursing veil. Her oval face with the intense blue eyes is set and solemn with the seriousness of her duty.

Woman and child approach the first bed. A hand rises and the woman grasps it.

The man speaks, and the girl turns to her mother. "He says he's happy you've come to see him."

"Tell him that I thank him for his courage, and that this cross is a token of my, and the king's, and our country's gratitude for his sacrifice."

As her mother hands her a small cross, Ileana translates her mother's words. As she speaks, she deftly loops a ribbon through the top of the cross and gently places it around the soldier's neck. Marie helps the man sit up, and Ileana places a plate of food on the tray beside the bed. The wounded soldier smiles and nods his thanks. He grabs his princess's hand and presses it to his cheek before the woman and her daughter move to the next bed.

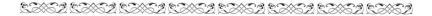

IT DIDN'T SEEM TO PHASE ILEANA AT ALL, as Marie noted the day after their visit to the nursing ward. "In the evening Mircea and Ileana played in my room as in the days of peace; it did me good to hear their happy, innocent voices, to watch their games."

A few days after Ileana's first visit to the hospital, she and Mircea woke up "not feeling well." Ileana recovered quickly—the illness didn't seem to touch her as badly as it did her brother. But as the days passed, and his eyes grew glassier as his temperature climbed, the doctors looked more and more somber.

Ileana with Mircea

After a long delay, they finally broke the news to the family: Mircea had typhoid fever.* Easily curable by antibiotics today, typhoid was a dread killer in the early days of the twentieth century.

Mircea was in agony. His temperature soared and he sank into delirium. He called constantly for his beloved sister Ileana. With her deep love of her brother, Ileana must have been terrified for the boy. He rallied, but then sank repeatedly over the next month. The family waited in anguish, listening to his screams as cool wet sheets were wrapped against him to try to bring the fever down. He lay, white against the white sheets, eyes upturned. Finally, at nine o'clock in the evening on November 2, 1916, his tiny hot hand clasped in his mother's, three-year-old Mircea died.

Queen Marie with Ileana and baby Mircea

The funeral was held in the church at Cotroceni Palace. White chrysanthemums glowed amid the lighted tapers, and Mircea was buried in the churchyard under the leafless trees on a dull November day.

In the days following Mircea's funeral, Ileana, heart aching, watched and learned. She absorbed a lesson in duty, responsibility, and strength that she never forgot. It stood her in good stead in the future, when her own desolation came.

With the closeness she always shared with Queen Marie, and her own love for Mircea, she knew how deep her mother's grief went. Yet amazingly, Marie, instead of turning inward and isolating herself, poured herself into her work with the wounded soldiers. After a grueling day at the hospital, she would return to Buftea at night to meet with her husband, King Ferdinand, and their chief advisor and closest friend, Prince Barbu Stirbey, to discuss the progress of the war and conditions at the front.

Ileana might have been a child—a seven-year-old—but she was perceptive and intelligent, and she watched her mother's reaction to the death of her son. From Marie's example, she learned to pour herself out for her country, to give even when there was nothing left, and to hide her deepest feelings in order that others might still lean on her. She learned, too, valuable lessons in how to go on, how to appear to live even when her own heart was torn from her.

Princess Ileana (top) with sisters Elisabeta and Mignon, brother Nicolas, and parents Queen Marie and King Ferdinand

CHAPTER THREE

Flight & Exile

Deliver me from my enemies, O Lord,
For to You I flee for refuge. (Psalm 142:9)

eep in the evening of the twenty-fifth of November, Ileana, her mother and sisters, and the court shivered on the Bucharest train platform. The cold winter wind blew hard and stiff, slicing through thick coats and warm stockings. People around her muttered about the cold and the icy wind, and worried about whether they would make it safely to Jassy.* The Germans were almost in Bucharest and they were bombing the train lines all around the city. Even in the train, it was chilly, and as it pulled out of the station Ileana must have wondered if she would ever see her home again.

They reached the new city safely, but for two weeks, the family, servants, and court lived in the crowded and cramped train. Even with long walks through the local countryside, and games and songs to cheer them, it was a boring and frightening wait until a house was found.

Despite being only seven years old, Ileana "was not too young to understand what was happening." Jassy, she realized, was a disaster in progress. If the war didn't destroy what was left of Romania, the conditions in Jassy might, by destroying the remainder of her people.

The city is located in the northeast of Romania, about ten miles from the border of Bessarabia—a region that had once been Romanian, but in

1916 was part of the crumbling Russian Empire. Jassy, the quiet capital of Moldavia, housed, in peacetime, about 60,000 residents.

All through November and December, over 230,000 Romanian refugees poured into the city, while the wounded continued to arrive from the front. No one had planned for an evacuation, so there was no organization, and Ileana saw that the small, quiet city was ill-equipped to handle so many newcomers.

People wandered the streets, searching desperately for somewhere to sleep and for food to keep them going. Hospitals were overwhelmed, and what few medical supplies did get through were held up for lack of organization to distribute them.

Conditions became even harsher as the worst winter in fifty years settled in. Deep snow blocked the train lines and roads into the city, preventing supplies from reaching Jassy. Coal was nonexistent, and people cut down the trees in the city parks for fuel.

With the king busy with the military situation, Queen Marie began to sort out the most pressing needs, Ileana and her other daughters at her side. They visited the overstrained hospitals daily, where they found a situation straight from hell.

"In a place meant only for three hundred, seven hundred have been herded together in barn-like constructions, without ventilation or light, with muddy floors which are nothing but stamped earth, the beds fixed one above the other. And stuffed into these, a crowd of unfortunate beings with every imaginable eye complaint, not to speak of several forms of typhus.* No place for isolating infectious diseases, and no sanitary arrangements of any kind."

The overcrowding meant that as many as three men shared a single bed. The lack of fuel had serious consequences—not only were the men shivering in the freezing and drafty wards, without either coal or wood to heat them, but they couldn't be cleaned, the wounds could not be washed and bandages couldn't be sterilized. Infection and pneumonia were everywhere, killing more than the battle wounds did.

On their return home after every trip, Ileana and her mother stepped into tubs of boiling hot water and shed their clothes, in order to kill the disease-bearing fleas and lice they'd picked up during their visits.

In the city, all through 1916 and 1917, the crisis continued. If the medical and heating situations weren't bad enough, the lack of food in the city made things that much worse, and not even the royal family was exempt.

"I can remember being always hungry," Ileana said, "and yet wishing I never need eat, for the limited amount of food we were able to get had limited variety." Beans were the staple, along with a monotonous repetition of "soup with scraps of horseflesh and cabbage, maize, a bit of black bread and black coffee made from dried acorns." Often, the food was so spoiled that in better times it would have been thrown out. As a result of the vitamin deficiencies she suffered, Ileana was to have health problems all her life.

Yet they were lucky, and Ileana knew it. The streets of Jassy were crowded with starving, homeless people, and it wrung her heart. During meals she begged guests and family for their bread, then later slipped down to the kitchen, where the cook made her a thermos of hot tea, or just hot water if there was nothing else. She packed a basket with the food she'd acquired and slipped out the door. She, and sometimes Mignon, wandered the streets of the city, distributing the tea and bread among the homeless and starving people.

As well-intentioned as it was, her charity didn't help much. People were dying in droves.

⬥⬥⬥⬥ Ileana Remembers ⬥⬥⬥⬥

For years I saw in nightmare dreams the funeral "procession" I so often saw as a child in Jassy: the bony horse drawing an ordinary farm cart loaded with dead bodies, piled as high as possible; a rough board put across the wagon bed to make a seat where beside the driver sat a priest in his vestments, and an army trumpeter to sound his call over the mass graves. One day while it passed our house I watched from a window, wondering how such a starved-looking animal could pull the heavy wagon. Suddenly the horse stopped and quite slowly collapsed between the shafts, dead. His fall overturned the wagon, and the naked bodies spilled stiffly out over the street. I remember catching sight of our Romanian cavalry guard rushing out to help as I turned away from the window to run for comfort to the little wooden horse I had brought with me from Bucarest—the favorite toy of my baby brother Mircea, who had died only a month before we were driven from our home.

I remember our Romanian guard also on the day the Bolshevik Revolution* was declared in Jassy. The house into which our family was crowded stood next to the Russian headquarters, and I looked out of my bedroom window to see the Russian officers lined up against their garden wall, while Russian enlisted men prepared to shoot them. Between our yard and theirs was a dividing wall, with wood stacked against it; and while I watched, frozen with horror, our guard, who had heard what was happening, came rushing around the house. Drawing their swords, they dashed up over the woodpile to the top of the wall and jumped into the Russian garden in time to rescue the officers—but not all scenes of violence ended so happily.

A SLIGHT RAY OF LIGHT PENETRATED THE GLOOM in January of 1917. Ileana's Aunt Ducky—her mother's favorite sister—arrived from St. Petersburg, Russia, along with presents for the family. Ileana delightedly received a paint box and a toy horse and cart, and the entire family were pleased with the good leather boots Ducky produced. It was like Christmas all over again.

Ducky also brought a trainload of provisions for the army and the hospitals. But news from Russia wasn't good, and the trouble was not confined to just the imperial family. Her news was confirmed when in March, a revolution broke out, forcing the tsar, Ileana's second cousin, to abdicate. The Russian Revolution* had begun, and it would have serious consequences for Romania and the royal family, both in this war and in years to come.

In Jassy, the situation continued to deteriorate. In such overcrowded, filthy conditions epidemics were inevitable. Typhoid fever and typhus raged through the city. It was only by the grace of God that neither Ileana nor her mother succumbed to either disease, for neither of them stopped visiting and comforting the wounded soldiers, or helping the homeless and starving civilians.

Through it all, Ileana continued to learn from her mother. Marie, with her basically optimistic outlook, her charm and outgoing personality, was determined not to let anyone see how truly desperate she felt the situation to be, or how devastated she was by Mircea's recent death.

Marie kept on, helping one when it was impossible to help many, helping a few when and where she could. No one except Ileana saw the queen's ongoing grief over her youngest son. At times, they cuddled on Marie's bed, "mingling their tears" while they talked of their beloved Mircea.

Ileana found her own respite from the pressure and the grief. She became best friends with the daughter of the court physician, Iona Perticari, and the girls spent hours playing dress-up and board games both in Ileana's house and at Iona Perticari's home just outside Jassy.

Nicky took his mother and sisters for car rides in the country in Bambino, his sports car. Ileana loved the rides, and Nicky, a bright and energetic sixteen-year-old, enjoyed taking her out.

Ileana and her mother both rode horseback as well, and one of their greatest pleasures was to take an afternoon and roam the hills around Jassy. Tango, an earth-colored roan pony with a long, flowing mane and tail whom Ileana adored, wasn't as fast as Marie's horse, so Marie would ride ahead and stop on a rise, waiting for her daughter to catch up. Tango would race as fast as he could, Ileana urging him on, her tall grey astrakhan* hat in danger of blowing off, her Cossack* dress blowing in the wind, eyes shining and cheeks flushed. As they caught their breath, they would gaze over the hills toward Bucharest and talk of all they'd left behind.

CHAPTER FOUR

Revolution & Surrender

Deliver me, O Lord, from the evil man, . . .
Who devised wrongdoing in their heart;
They arrayed themselves for war all day long. (Psalm 139:2–3)

he winds of revolution were blowing across Russia. They gusted through nearby Bessarabia and wafted into the Romanian army. Without a doubt, they had fertile soil upon which to drop the seeds of sedition and revolt.

For years, the common Romanians had clamored for more land owner-ship and more say in public affairs. As the revolution spread to the Russian troops, it infected the Romanian soldiery, who logically figured that if they were fighting for their country's land, why couldn't they own a part of it and have a say in the way it was run?

With the structure of the Romanian government, the royal family had very little real power to effect change, but this didn't stop King Ferdinand from traveling to the front to address the troops. In fact, His Majesty's prom-ises for agricultural and political reform once the war was over earned King Ferdinand the title "King of the Peasants."

Ileana was proud of her father for having spoken up for the peasants, and for the rest of her life it was something she recalled with evident pleasure.

Through the summer of 1917, Ileana led a somewhat nomadic existence. Her mother, while adamant about duty, also recognized that Ileana was a young child. To refresh her from the day-to-day horrors of the war, she allowed Ileana to divide her summer between an isolated valley northwest of Jassy, the hospital at Ghidigeni with her sister Mignon, and Marie's private retreat of Cotofenesti.

Ileana returned with her mother from Cotofenesti in September to find that, with the American declaration of war against Germany, the American ambassador had arrived in Jassy, bringing with him a large contingent of Red Cross workers and supplies, headed by Col. Henry Anderson.

At seven years of age, most children spend their time in school, but Ileana was tutored at home. Reading, writing, and arithmetic did not teach her what she needed to know about being a princess, though, and her mother furthered Ileana's royal education by allowing her to accompany her on hospital rounds and to work as a translator for Col. Anderson and his team.

Autumn was a period of grueling uncertainty, fear, and worry. While Ileana's parents didn't hide unpleasantness from their children, neither did they go out of their way to put frightening news in front of them. But even the dullest of children, which Ileana was not, would have known the situation was grim.

In October, Lenin and the Bolsheviks came to power in Moscow. In Romania, Russian troop morale fell even further, and the Romanian soldiers couldn't stand against the superior numbers of the enemy. Surrender was imminent.

Christmas was a perfect time for whatever festivity they could make. But Marie was also a realist and hadn't wanted to raise hopes in Ileana. She warned her youngest daughter not to expect the arrival of Father Christmas. "He wouldn't be able to get over the German lines," is the way she put it to the eight-year-old.

Regardless of Father Christmas's travel problems, Ileana wanted to give a tea party. She and her sisters cobbled together a tree and invited her French, American, and English co-workers.

At the party, Ileana confided her mother's news about Father Christmas to her American friends. They were shocked and refused to believe it. Santa

Claus could go anywhere, Col. Anderson stated. The measly Germans couldn't stop him! Father Christmas would visit Ileana, they were positive of it. So reassured, Ileana went on to serve the plum pudding, the highlight of the meal.

Imagine This

Exhausted after the excitement of the Christmas party, it takes Ileana a few minutes to waken fully. Giggles and hushed voices from the foot of her bed. Are some of the women in the crowded room playing a game? It's so late. But the voices are too low for women. They sound like men. A muffled laugh, a "Shhhh! You'll wake her!"

That is Col. Anderson! What is he—half opening her eyes, remaining as still as she can, Ileana looks to the foot of her bed. Crowding around the stocking she'd hung from the bedpost are at least a dozen officers. She hears her mother's chuckle as the officers fill her stocking.

So, Father Christmas would make it through the German lines, eh? She smiles to herself as she remembers the outraged protests during the party. Somehow, seeing the men gather around her bed, doing their best to keep her belief alive, she is more convinced than ever, even though her belief is not in the traditional Father Christmas. She knows now that the bountiful spirit of both Father Christmas and St. Nicholas has always been with her family and these generous, kind friends. She watches until they finish and tiptoe out. It is amazing how quiet such big heavy boots can be, she thinks as she closes her eyes, smiling.

In the morning, she grabs the stocking and upends it over the bedcovers. What a strange collection! A tobacco pouch of leather—she can keep her little bits of money in that one, and one of rubber. A wooden cigarette case, an American gold coin, and oh! such riches! A small chocolate bar, all to herself. A regimental badge from one of the British men, and tiny British and American flags, an orange and several nuts make up the bulk of her gifts. She smiles, happy, but aware she can't give her secret away and thank the officers—they have to believe their trick worked!

CHAPTER FIVE

The Tide Turns; Family Troubles

My son, do not despise the instruction of the Lord,
Neither grow weary under His reproof.
For whom the Lord loves He instructs,
And chastises every son He receives.
(Proverbs 3:11, 12)

he shortages continued into January 1918, and even though "nothing is to be had, not even a flower," Ileana was delighted with the few gifts she received on her ninth birthday.

The new year brought no end to the pressure—the war situation was so bad that on March 4, the Romanian government finally surrendered.

Imagine This

Ileana clings to her mother's hand as the last of the passengers climb on the train. It's dark outside the circle of lights in the station, and their breath puffs out in imitation of the steam from the locomotive. On this night, which has just become March 9, Ileana's chill is as much from inside as it is from the freezing night air. She stands, Mama on one side, Nicky on the other, and Lisabeta behind her, tall and brave, waving sadly to the members of the Allied missions who are leaving on this late night train.

It's just after midnight, and they've all come from what felt like the strangest party ever. As she shivers and tries not to cry, Ileana thinks back to earlier that evening, when in spite of the sorrow and the tears during the goodbye speeches, the conversation flowed easily. The recitations by Ventura, one of the foremost actresses of the Romanian stage, were brilliant (at least according to the adults—Ileana thought they were boring), and George Enescu, the gifted young musician, played exquisitely. It felt like the best party ever and a funeral all mixed up together. Even while people were laughing at jokes, she could hear the sorrow underneath; she watched as people would suddenly leave the room for a few minutes, then return as if nothing were wrong. Adults are strange—but she knows that appearances have to be kept up, and a brave face put on the worst disasters—even surrender.

She fingers the purse in her pocket and smiles, still pleased and proud in spite of the sorrow. She thinks about how happy she'd been when Col. Anderson called for silence partway through the evening. He made a little speech about how welcome the Red Cross delegation had felt and how much help they'd been given by the court and the royal family. And then he called her up and said that Ileana's help had been among the greatest, and that all of them had been impressed by her dedication and by the love she had for the work they did. And then, if that weren't enough, he'd presented her with a pouch of money. She hadn't counted it yet, but there was a large stack of bills. He told her that he was giving it to her to continue the good work they'd all been involved in, and he trusted that she would know best how to use it.

And now, she thinks, her smile fading, they have to leave. All of them. Her mother explained on the way to the station—it's part of the surrender terms the Germans are imposing on the Romanians. Marie says that the government disapproves, but she persuaded the king to bring the whole family along to the station to say goodbye to the British, French, and Americans.

Ileana's sight blurs as she gazes into the train windows, waving and calling out. She can't tell who is waving back—is it Col. Anderson? She blinks and sees him blow her a kiss. Sniffing hard, she catches it and tucks it into her worn, patched coat, then blows him one back. She's supposed to be brave, she's supposed to show how strong a Romanian princess is, but she can't help the tears trickling down her face as the train begins to move, and her friends and allies move away, leaving her and her country bereft.

THE ONLY ALLY TO REMAIN BEHIND was the Canadian Col. Joe Boyle. He was there when the Allied missions left Jassy at midnight. It was his presence that allowed both Ileana and Marie to get through the evening without breaking down completely. In the dark days following the signing of the peace treaty, Col. Boyle's staunch support of her mother and her country won Ileana's heart, and she came to know him as "Uncle Joe."

Colonel Joseph Whiteside Boyle was, even for those days, a striking and unusual man. He became one of Ileana's closest friends, and their friendship would last until Boyle's death in 1923. Born in 1867, he was in his fifties when he first arrived in Romania after a long and adventurous life.

Boyle had made a fortune in the Klondike* during the 1890s gold rush. When war broke out, he was too old to enlist—instead, he raised a machine-gun unit* from the Klondike area. But this wasn't enough—he wanted to be in on the action. To make it up to him and to recognize his efforts, the Canadian government made Boyle an honorary lieutenant colonel, and he traveled to Britain to be near his men. He had acted independently all his life, and to him, orders were suggestions, to be ignored if they didn't suit him.

The British, unsure of what to do with such a fellow, sent him to Russia to help with the rail transportation problems there, while they and the Canadians tried to figure out who was in charge of him.

He met the Romanians when his work with the railroads took him into Bessarabia. At the Romanian government's request, he traveled to Russia and managed not only to rescue a number of the Romanian crown jewels and important papers, but also to "liberate" and bring back several train-carloads of supplies. In January 1918 he had flown to Odessa, boarded a Russian ship on which there were a large number of Romanian prisoners, and through a combination of daring and bluff, managed to save them all from exile or worse.

Queen Marie met and thanked him personally for his work and brav-ery, and for the rest of his life, he became a loyal and devoted friend to her and Ileana.

⁂

EVEN IN DEFEAT, Ileana and Marie could not be cowed. Ileana certainly didn't know the terms of the armistice, but the German actions told her they were harsh and punitive. The Germans sent occupying troops but left the royal family and the government intact, realizing that to remove them or harm them would bring full-scale revolt from the Romanian citizens.

The occupation forces were systematically looting the country. They instituted forced labor for all peasants, and deported, imprisoned, or just plain shot everyone who disobeyed. They took over the oil fields, rivers, and farms, and controlled all communications. While they didn't remove the royal family from power or interfere with King Ferdinand in many ways, they distributed propaganda condemning them.

The old, pre-surrender parliament had resigned in protest at the mea-sures of the German occupation. The new one, believing that the Central Powers would win the war, went along with everything their masters wanted. Soon after the treaty had been signed, the cabinet members of the new government came to breakfast with the royal family.

Both Marie and Ileana had to be present, yet neither wanted anything to do with these men. As a young, disregarded child, Ileana was able to slip away quickly, but Marie had to remain, put on her most diplomatic face, and be the queen. Her daughter sympathized, and afterwards asked her, "How could you stand it, to be there?"

Over the course of the spring of 1918, Marie retired to her little house at Cotofenesti. There, she and Ileana ignored the government in Jassy and kept themselves from the distressing occupation of the country. Marie con-tinued with her charitable work, visiting the villages and hospitals. Ileana accompanied her and made friends with the local children. She later re-membered the spring and summer of 1918 as one of the happiest, most con-tented periods of her life.

She got to know Dimitru and Stanca, a brother and sister, and their clos-est friends, four brothers, all named Ion. They rambled through the hills, waded in the creeks and rivers, and climbed the trees in the warm spring sun. When they tired, they would return to her home and sit in the dappled shade of a lime tree, the scent filling their noses, while Marie told them stories of her life in Britain and Malta. And the children would discuss their faith and the Church. Ileana would tell them about the monasteries and what the lives of the monks and nuns were like. Lively and intelligent, the other children questioned her about what their faith meant, and the discussions would occupy entire afternoons.

They did chores, Ileana working alongside them as they tended to the pigs, the sheep, and a beautiful white cow the Ions owned. She was so taken with the cow that she named it "the Holy White Cow of India."

Ileana loved to visit their village to help Baba Elisabeta, Stanca and Dimitru's grandmother. She spent hours with the other villagers and dropped in to talk to Marie, an invalid girl suffering from tuberculosis.

She spent her entire time in Cotofenesti speaking Romanian, and for the rest of her life was grateful to her friends for giving her what she called "the real foundation" for her knowledge of the Romanian language. In addition, her friends gave her the roots of her lifelong devotion to Romania and its people, for she could never separate the country from the faces of those she played and worked with over this and other summers in the years ahead.

As the summer wore on, the entire family reunited and moved to Bicaz, to the Crown Estate house in the Carpathian mountains. Uncle Joe, between diplomatic and war-related assignments, was a frequent visitor. But in July, after he suffered a severe stroke, Marie insisted he stay with them to recover.

Ileana spent hours with her beloved Uncle Joe as he recuperated, talking to him, reading to him, and listening to him recite the verses of Canadian poet Robert Service. The strong rhythm and vivid images in "The Cremation of Sam McGee" and "The Shooting of Dan McGrew" would have appealed to her at nine years of age.

When he was well enough to move about, the two visited the villages around Bicaz. In one village, he bought a house, and he and Ileana had a wonderful time helping the workmen fix it up. He donated the house, in Ileana's name, to three refugee families when it was finished. With Ileana's company, he supervised repairs to buildings all over the valley, located and delivered supplies to the starving peasants, and spent huge sums of money trying to ease some of the poverty and want.

Boyle's active generosity to her countrymen impressed Ileana, and along with her mother's work, taught her valuable lessons in altruism and charity. These lessons were underlined by her visits to the monasteries in the valley, where she learned from and prayed with the monks and nuns, soaked in the serenity of God's presence, and learned to rely on Him and trust in Him for everything from the games after lunch to the problems of her country.

❧❊❧

BUT ALL WAS NOT COMPLETELY PEACEFUL. Outside their quiet valley and victimized country, the war still raged. By the summer of 1918, in the West the balance of power was beginning to shift. The Allies, with the addition of American troops in 1917, began to win battles, and the tide of the war finally began to turn.

East of them, in Russia, the revolution continued, and late in the summer, Ileana's family received the shocking news of the murder of the tsar and his family—her cousins.

Then, on September 15, real disaster struck, both for the family and the country. Prince Carol, heir to the throne, deserted his regiment, renounced his right to the succession, and with his lover, Zizi Lambrino, eloped. They were found in Odessa in Bessarabia. In spite of Carol and Ileana's closeness, it's unlikely that young Ileana knew of his plans.

Once he returned to Romania, he was imprisoned in Bistritza Monastery near Bicaz, and it wasn't until early 1919, after constant pressure from the king, the prime minister, and Col. Boyle, that Carol finally renounced his marriage and agreed to its annulment.

❧❊❧

IN EARLY NOVEMBER, while the country was between elected governments but still under German occupation, King Ferdinand, now back in Jassy, proclaimed the land and voting reforms he'd promised to his soldiers a few years before. The news was greeted with jubilation, both in Romania and among the Allied troops who had just crossed the Danube. It was November 1918, and the First World War was almost over. The puppet government had guessed wrong, and the Allies were winning against Germany and its allies.

Queen Marie, Ileana, and the rest of the household left Bicaz at the beginning of November, arriving in Jassy on November 11. At the train station they almost literally fell into the arms of the reception committee, composed of members of the new government, the king and allied representatives, returned to Romania in the face of the victory. Ileana was as overjoyed as the rest as they learned of the end of the war and the defeat of the Germans.

≈≈≈ ≈≈≈ ≈≈≈ Imagine This ≈≈≈ ≈≈≈ ≈≈≈

Ileana can't hear what Mignon is saying, the roar of the crowd is so loud, but she nods anyway. Ahead of her, the horses, four of them, prance and toss their heads, as though they too are glad that the family is back in Bucharest.

The signal is given and the carriage moves forward, just behind Carol's regiment. Ileana's parents will follow at the very end, on their own horses. For a moment, she wishes she could be beside them on Tango, free and able to ride, but this is as good, and she can enjoy seeing the streets and squares and the people she's missed for two long years.

The route winds from the train station just on the outskirts of the city right to the center square, and Ileana is overwhelmed by the size of the crowd. Every single person who lives within miles of Bucharest must be here today, and all of them are shouting and cheering and singing at the top of their lungs! It feels as if the houses and roads are shouting with joy to see the royal family back where they belong. Every building is draped with bunting; every lamppost sports a flag. They flutter from the housetops and in the hand of every child. It's a sea, a tidal wave of red, yellow, and blue.

The joy in the faces of the people lining the streets brings an answering joy to Ileana, and she redoubles her waving, both hands up and out, as she tries to encompass them all. But for all the joy in their eyes and the lightness of their faces, she can see the suffering as well: clothes are ragged, not just on the beggars, but on everyone. Many don't have coats and shiver in the freezing November air. The faces on the edge of the route are thin, pinched, and yellow in the bright winter sun. Through the decoration covering the buildings, Ileana can see the devastation. Shattered walls, broken windows, bullet holes and scorch marks in brick, and broken-up pavement confirm the shadows of hardship she sees in the faces of the people around her.

But today is a day of joy, and she cannot dwell on the past. Ileana smiles and waves, her happiness at being home at least equal to the joy of her people's welcome.

Section II

Teenage Princess

Ileano

1922

TIMELINE 1918–1930

YEAR	COUNTRY	EVENT
1918	Romania	Prince Carol abdicates heirship, elopes with Zizi Lambrino; passage of land reform bills promised by King Ferdinand
1919	Romania	Queen Marie travels with her daughters, including Ileana, to France; formation of Romania Mare—Greater Romania
	France	Treaty negotiations begin at Versailles in France
1920	France	Treaty of Versailles ratified by most countries—WWI officially ends
	Canada	Arthur Meighan becomes prime minister
	Britain	Irish problems break out into violence
1921	Romania	Marriage of Elizabeth (Lisabeta) to Prince George of Greece; marriage of Carol to Princess Helen (Sitta) of Greece; birth of Mihai (Michael), Crown Prince of Romania, to Carol and Sitta
	Canada	Insulin discovered
		William Lyon McKenzie King becomes prime minister
	USA	Warren Harding becomes president
	Germany	Adolf Hitler assumes leadership of National Socialist German Workers Party
1922	Romania	Marriage of Marie (Mignon) to King Alexander of Serbia; Coronation of King Ferdinand and Queen Marie of Romania Mare
	Italy	Benito Mussolini becomes dictator
	Germany	Out-of-control inflation—$1.00 US equals 10,000 Reich Marks
1923	Romania	Revised constitution enacted into law, recognizing Orthodoxy as the state religion and establishing a democratic electoral system
	USA	Calvin Coolidge becomes president after Warren Harding dies
	Britain	Prince Albert (King George VI) & Lady Elizabeth Bowes-Lyon married (parents of the present Queen Elizabeth II)

YEAR	COUNTRY	EVENT
1923	Germany	Beer Hall Putsch attempted and failed, Hitler arrested and sentenced to prison; 60 million Reich Marks = $1.00 US
1925	Romania	Ileana, at fifteen years of age, delivers her first public address to the Romanian Girl Reserves; Ileana travels to Britain for a year of boarding school; Prince Carol abdicates and flees Romania with Elena Lupescu
1926	America	Ileana accompanies Queen Marie on railroad tour of US and Canada
	Britain	Princess Elizabeth, later Queen Elizabeth II, born; labor unrest and general strike
	USA	Celebrates 150 years of nationhood
	Canada	Mackenzie King again becomes prime minister
1927	Romania	King Ferdinand, "King of the Peasants," dies; succeeded by his six-year-old grandson Mihai and a regency council
1928	World	Worldwide depression begins
	Romania	Princess Helen (Sitta) divorces Carol
	USA	Amelia Earhart first woman to fly across the Atlantic
	Britain	Discovery of penicillin by Alexander Fleming
1929	Romania	Carol enters serious discussions with brother Prince Nicholas and Prime Minister Iuliu Maniu about returning to Romania
	USA, Canada, Britain	Great Depression begins; in US, Herbert Hoover becomes president
1930	Romania	Carol returns and forces abdication of his son Mihai, now aged nine
	Canada	R. B. Bennett becomes prime minister
	Britain	Princess Margaret Rose, sister of Queen Elizabeth II, born
	Germany	Great Depression hits, worsening already bad economic situation

CHAPTER SIX

A 'Real' Princess

Her ways are good ways,
And all her paths are in peace.
(Proverbs 3:19)

he next years were like a dream for Ileana in spite of Romania's troubles. For perhaps the first time in her memory, the nine-year-old lived a life most people think princesses live all the time.

She wrote that her time after the war was taken up with "work and study, with none of the freedom and gay social occasions that are taken for granted by teenagers in the United States." Maybe so, but if she got too bored, or the weather was nice, she could always charm her tutor into a walk in the woods.

Ileana's basically sunny nature enabled her to find joy in the most dreary lessons and boring dinner companions, and some of the duties that came her way were positively enchanting. It wasn't long after the family had returned to Bucharest that she learned that she, her mother, and her sisters were going to Paris. King Ferdinand, recognizing his wife's strengths as well as her international popularity, asked her to travel to Paris and act as an unofficial representative for her country. She and her daughters were elated.

Besides working for Romania, Marie had her own motives for wanting her daughters with her. Lisabeta and Mignon were of marriageable age: Lisabeta was twenty-four and Mignon eighteen. With peace a reality, it was

45

time they became reacquainted with Europe's other eligible royals. In addition, they wanted to further their educations.

Ileana glowed with excitement and happiness through the entire train trip. But none of them were expecting the reception they got when they arrived in the French capital. Marie and her daughters were mobbed every time they appeared in public, from the moment they arrived at the train station to their leave-taking to travel to London, England.

They didn't have to shop—the most fashionable designers and retailers in Paris courted Marie and her girls, anxious to reap the rewards of dressing the most famous family in Europe. The women were happy to oblige. Although none of them, except Mignon, were obsessed with fashion, it had been five years since they'd had anything new at all. Ileana had worn her best outfit when she arrived in Paris—a dress made from her mother's old coat. While her mother talked to politicians and diplomats, Ileana chose new clothing and saw the sights. And together they attended formal public dinners, private parties, and luncheon engagements.

The visit was a success on more than one front. Romania received most of what she had been promised at war's end, including Transylvania, Bukovina, and Bessarabia, and the country was recognized as Romania Mare,* Greater Romania. Marie also talked the American Red Cross into sending not only train cars full of desperately needed supplies and food, but workers as well, who traveled back with Marie and Ileana. It was just the two of them returning home; Mignon and Lisabeta had stayed at schools in England and Paris.

In June of 1919, Ileana returned to France "for a cure." While we don't know the details of her stay there, or what the cure was for, it was probably related to the stresses and strains of the war. In photographs taken during the war, she appears as a thin child with large solemn eyes in an oval face framed by chin-length dark hair. She looks like a child who has seen too much sorrow.

In addition to the joy the war robbed her of, she was left with nutritional deficiencies that would plague her for the rest of her years and necessitate numerous operations. Most of her life was spent in a great deal of pain. It may be that this "rest cure" was the first evidence of the weaknesses the war had left her with.

Ileana was back in Romania by the late summer, and that autumn, the Red Cross finished its emergency work. The government persuaded the workers to stay on another year, with the bulk of their work focused on child welfare and strengthening international Red Cross ties. Here Ileana was able to use the money Col. Anderson had left with her: at ten years of age, she took on the leadership of the Romanian Junior Red Cross.* She took the reins with eagerness; as her mother said, she was fast growing into an enthusiastic social worker.

This wasn't easy for Ileana. Despite her training, she was painfully shy. Only her deep need to help and the fact that it was her duty to work for her people enabled her to overcome the feeling of being awkward and incompetent. It was so hard for her to put herself forward that she often fainted with the stress of it, and she never completely overcame her fear of speaking in public.

Even though Ileana's life improved over these years, and she had almost twenty years of happiness, the seeds of a deep and cutting betrayal were sown during the immediate postwar years.

Her brother Carol had always had a problematic relationship with his family. He alternately loved and hated his mother, was jealous of his siblings and of their popularity with the Romanian people. Ileana, it seemed, was the only one he truly loved, and even that love was clouded by his jealousy of her closeness to their mother and her growing popularity with their people.

Throughout late 1918 and 1919, Carol continued to cause controversy and scandal, culminating, late in the summer of 1919, in his refusal to join his regiment in a war against Hungary's invasion of Transylvania. Marie wrote him a scathing letter, accusing him of betraying his country, and told him to "be a man and go with your regiment."

Furious and resentful, Carol reached a breaking point, and he again renounced his claim to the throne. All through that summer and fall, Marie, Ferdinand, members of the government, and Uncle Joe worked to change Carol's mind.

Ileana supported her mother and defended her to Carol. As well, she tried her best to persuade him to stand by his birthright and do his duty. As much as he loved her, Carol found her defense of their mother's position intolerable, and although he finally fell into line, whatever love he'd had for Marie and Ileana was replaced with a burning, angry grudge that he nursed for the rest of his life. Years later, he made them pay dearly for their insistence that he do his duty.

In the main, though, the years from 1919 until the end of the 1920s (when Ileana was from ten to twenty years of age) were happy ones. She continued with her schoolwork and got more involved in the work of the family, as well as celebrating its enlargement through her siblings' marriages and children. Prince George, Crown Prince of Greece, had been in love with Ileana's older sister Lisabeta for years, and on a family vacation set up for the purpose, George's constant faithfulness won Elisabeta over. In addition, during the same vacation, Carol fell head over heels in love with George's sister, Princess Helen.

In 1920, Queen Marie was given a gift that would have a huge impact on Ileana, and would, perhaps more than any other place in Romania, come to be identified with her. After Marie's return from Paris, during the upheaval of Carol's messy private life, the city of Brasov* presented as a thank-you gift to Queen Marie a rundown, beaten-up fortress located a few miles south of the city, near the village of Bran.

❧❧❧ Imagine This ❧❧❧

The trip to Bran has been long and difficult, due to the conditions of the roads in the steep mountains, but as the car approaches the tiny village, Ileana, just turned eleven, gasps and Marie leans forward to tell the driver to stop the car.

Mother and daughter step out and gaze in stupefied amazement at the fortress looming over the valley ahead of them.

Sitting on top of a steep, rocky crag, it gives, despite its blinding white walls, the impression of a dark, brooding presence. The sheer walls, turrets, and gabled roofs state clearly that this is a fortress, intended to repel all who would attempt to breach its defenses. It stands over the valley and the village of Bran in solitary splendor.

"It's marvelous, Mama," breathes Ileana. "I wonder what it looks like inside."

Bran Castle

"I always thought it called to me," replies her mother. "Years ago, when I was traveling through here, I saw it sitting in such heartbreaking solitude. I want to turn it into a home and give it a heart."

"Then how perfect that Brasov has given it to you!" says Ileana. "I want to help."

"Then you shall. Let's go on and see what it looks like." They climb back into the car and complete the trip to the castle. Though it is sadly neglected and run down, both Marie and Ileana are taken with the charming, eccentric interior of the thirteenth-century castle. While there are only four floors to the building, no more than two rooms on a single floor are on the same level. The inner courtyard is dirty and dingy, with leaves and garbage from years of neglect. The interior is dark, not due to lack of light, but from the discoloration of the walls and the darkening of the woodwork.

"Look here," says Marie. "We could transform this area into a lovely fourth-floor terrace, where we could sit at the end of the day and gaze over the village and into the mountains beyond."

Both women feel immediately at home, and know that wherever else in Romania they may live, their hearts will always be here, at Bran Castle.

IN EARLY 1921, within a space of two weeks (and with special permission from the Orthodox patriarchs), Elisabeth and George were married in Romania, followed by Carol and Helen's wedding in Greece.

After a busy spring, the royal family could have been expected to take a rest, but the fall brought even more celebrations. In October, Helen gave birth prematurely (almost dying in the process) to Carol's son and the heir to the throne, Mihai (or Michael).

Also, King Alexander of Serbia asked for Mignon's hand in marriage that fall. She accepted, and they were married in Serbia on June 8, 1922.

But the biggest event in everyone's life that year was the coronation of Ileana's parents at Alba Julia, in Transylvania. The delay was understandable. Romania had been on the verge of war when Ferdinand took the throne in August of 1916, and his first major action was to declare for the Allied cause. Even though the treaty negotiations in Paris after the war had unified Romania in its ancient boundaries, the country was almost penniless, and could not afford the expense of a formal coronation until 1922.

Imagine This

Ileana's attention is torn between the crowds on either side of the procession where she's walking, her parents walking behind her, and her gorgeous cloth-of-gold gown. The thirteen-year-old fingers the blue velvet mantle, delighting still in the new and luxurious fabric.

The Liturgy* today doesn't absorb her. She's too excited and proud at the fact that her parents are finally being crowned. After the service is over, she and the court and the rest of the dignitaries leave the church and walk to the center of town, where 300,000 people crowd the streets. They gather in a cordoned-off space around the enormous dais set in the center of the square. It's covered in brightly covered carpets, with a huge canopy to keep the autumn sun off the king and queen. The entire scene is a rainbow of colors, glittering, shining, and glowing even more than the fall leaves.

The grin of joy and pride threatens to wrap entirely around Ileana's head as she watches her parents slowly mount the dais, then pause while a royal purple mantle is placed on King Ferdinand's shoulders and a brilliant gold mantle draped on Queen Marie. The Patriarch intones the prayers, including praise to God's glory, gratitude for His blessings upon Romania and the royal family, and pleas that He will support and sustain the king in his Christian and beneficent rule over his beloved country. Ileana's voice joins all the others in a heartfelt "Amen!"

Then comes the moment. The King, taking the heavy iron crown from the priest, raises it slowly and lowers it upon his own head. Marie kneels before him and is crowned by her king and husband. He helps her to her feet, and they embrace while the crowd cheers—none more enthusiastically than their Ileana.

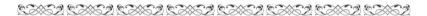

Queen Marie   King Ferdinand

CHAPTER SEVEN

Learning the Royal Ropes

Lay hold of my instruction; do not let go,
But guard it for yourself as your life.
(Proverbs 4:12)

Between the weddings and the coronation, Ileana wasn't idle. In addition to her regular lessons, she attended the School for Physical Education in Bucharest. Classes started at seven in the morning, and afterward, it was off to her tutor or whatever official event demanded her presence.

Dinner was never an intimate family affair. It was formal, which required evening dress, and was an extension of the king and queen's work, where they continued to entertain politicians, diplomats, and journalists. In addition, Marie was an extroverted woman who loved having people around her and would invite anyone she took a fancy to for dinner.

After dinner, Ileana would change again, into one of the uniforms required by the groups to which she belonged, and set off to one of the social service organizations that were springing up all over Romania.

In addition to her ongoing work with the Junior Red Cross, she was involved in the Girl Reserves of the YWCA* and spent uncounted hours with the other members—factory workers, shop clerks, and secretaries as well as the daughters of courtiers and university students. Much of their time was spent alternately in the slums of Bucharest—helping the poor and those most affected by the war, repairing the damage the bombs and battles had wrought—and in the convents and monasteries around the capital city.

In the summer of 1924, Ileana was introduced to her mother's latest renovation project. Marie bought an old millhouse and surrounding land near Balcic, a coastal town on the Black Sea not far from the Bulgarian border, in the Southern Dobrudja. Ileana, always an avid swimmer, was enchanted by the location—right on the shore. Bran and Balcic became Ileana's two favorite places. In the one, she was close to the monasteries and mountains she loved, and in the other, she could indulge her passion for the sea. These two places, more than any others, claimed her heart, and she returned to them again and again, whenever she could.

The following summer Ileana talked her parents into allowing her to attend school in England for a year. She wanted to be sure in her own mind that she had earned whatever honors she was given through her own hard work, not just because she was the princess of Romania. So in September, at sixteen years of age, Ileana enrolled at Mignon's old school: Heathfield, at Ascot in England.

Initially, it wasn't as successful an experiment as she'd hoped. The other girls in the school were from the British upper classes, but they weren't royal. Ileana didn't care, but they did. In addition, she was Romanian, and her mother's British blood counted for less than nothing. Ileana was excluded, gossiped about, and cruelly teased.

She had some solace because of her family connections. She spent short holidays with the British royal family and her brother Nicky, who was about to leave Eton and join the British Royal Navy. Her old friend, Ion Antonescu, visited her as well, enjoying his time with her as much as he had during the war in Jassy.

Even so, she was hurt beyond imagining, and ached through the first part of her year there while *Ileana in England, 1923* she tried to ignore the taunts, the cruel imitations of her accent, and the cold shoulders. She put her head down and got on with her work. She reveled in her art classes, where her inborn talent was honed and trained, and where, for a time, she could forget her loneliness and the coldness of her classmates. She drew, painted, and sculpted. She learned to carve wood. She sewed, embroidered, and knitted with enjoyment and talent; and in an effort to combat her still-crippling shyness, she took elocution lessons.

Music was not successful. Ileana was an educated listener, thanks to her mother's influence and her exposure to the cream of the talented Romanian musicians, but she couldn't sing or play an instrument. She enjoyed her gym classes, doing well in all sports.

At the time, the Guiding Movement,* begun in England by Lord Baden-Powell, was just sixteen years old—the same age as Ileana—and growing at a tremendous rate. She became a Guide while at school and was so enthusiastic that she took every course they offered, especially their leadership training courses. When she returned to Romania, she declared, she would help set up the Guides for Romanian girls.

Part of the Girl Guides included practical nursing training, and Ileana took those courses as well. It was, she quickly realized, something she felt born to do. She absorbed everything they could teach her and hungered for more. Nursing suited her. Helping the homeless and watching her mother's charitable works had taught her to help those who were hurt and ailing, and nursing was a perfect outlet for her.

Through her entire time in England, Ileana tried to treat everyone fairly, no matter how they hurt her. She drew on the lessons she'd learned at the dinner table when her mother had been taunted and insulted by Queen Elizabeth, and in watching her mother deal with the hated occupation forces at the end of World War I, as well as her own experiences in the official duties she'd always had to fulfill. She honed her ability to keep a serene and calm exterior, to hide what she really felt, so that the girls wouldn't see how hurt and lonely she was.

In late November of 1925, her brother Carol arrived in England for the funeral of the Queen Mother Alexandra, his and Ileana's second cousin. Marie and Ferdinand sent him to represent their family, partly because, once again, he was causing scandal and heartbreak.

Carol visited Ileana both during the funeral and afterward at her school, and proposed that they travel home together for Christmas.

Imagine This

Ileana glances at the clock on the bedside table, and a thread of worry stains her thoughts. Carol should be here by now—he said he'd arrive before lunch, and it's almost noon.

Restless, she stands to pace just as a knock sounds.

"Telephone call for you, *your highness,*" says Julie, one of Ileana's classmates.

"Thank you, Julie." Ileana conceals her hurt, still acute after three months of the taunts and icy disdain the English girls show her.

"Expecting a call from your majesty Mumsie?" Julie asks, her lip curled.

"I hope it's my brother. He's supposed to pick me up and we're to go home together for Christmas, but he's late. I hope nothing's happened," Ileana replies. A worried frown creases her forehead and the fear comes through in her voice.

"Oh, what could happen to a prince of the realm of Romania!" Julie responds. "Surely your army would protect him!"

"There are always enemies. Things are not stable in Romania."

Julie looks shocked and reaches out to touch Ileana's arm. "Oh," she says in a rush, "I'm sure it's all right. He's probably just missed his train. That's all it'll be."

The phone call is from Carol.

"There's been an emergency, Ileana. I have to go to Paris. A friend is in terrible trouble. I've taken care of all the arrangements for you to get home."

"But Carol—" Ileana grips the receiver. Disappointment and hurt crash over her. She had so been looking forward to this! Days and days of visiting together, talking and laughing. He'd promised to show her the latest pictures of Mihai, now two years old, and to listen to all her tales of school. He was so kind and caring. He'd have joked with her and made her feel special, and as though the loneliness didn't matter.

"I'm sorry, but this really is an emergency. I can't tell you any more—it's not my disaster to speak of, but please try to understand, sister."

Ileana summons all her resources. "Of course, Carol, I understand. We'll just have to meet some other time."

Relief gusts through his voice. "You're a terrific sister, Ileana. Thank you. I've got the trip laid out for you and the tickets have probably already arrived. I'll see you at home just as soon as this is taken care of, and we'll have a great talk. All right?" Without waiting for her assent, he hangs up.

WHEN SHE ARRIVED IN BUCHAREST, Ileana walked into a storm of scandal and outrage. After the happy, hopeful beginning of their marriage, Helen and Carol had grown apart. He had taken a mistress, Elena Lupescu. Just after Carol had departed for Queen Alexandra's funeral, Elena had left for Paris. Carol's "emergency" trip had been to join her.

He and Elena Lupescu had planned the entire thing, right down to visiting Ileana. Knowing that he would be arrested if word leaked out, he gave his promise to Ileana as a smokescreen to deflect suspicion. He never intended to escort her home. She must have been furious and deeply hurt at his use of her. Carol didn't care. Reunited with his latest passion, he once again renounced his claim to the throne. This time, Marie and Ferdinand stood firm and declared that it was best to let him go.

Ileana was devastated. In spite of the divisions between them, she loved Carol and wanted him to come home and do his duty, to be the man she knew he could be; but even her appeals were met by her parents with firm refusal. It was the third time, and for all of them, that was the final straw, but for Ileana it hurt as deeply as his betrayal of her.

CHAPTER EIGHT

Travel & Loss

*But if we hope for what we do not see, we eagerly wait for it
with perseverance. (Romans 8:25)*

n spite of Carol's treatment of her, Ileana returned to Britain
after the holidays and finished her year in school. She proved
to herself what she needed to: she could hold her own, earn her
honors through her own hard work, and gain the respect of her teachers.
More importantly, she had, through her warm charm and patient serenity,
finally cracked the icy disdain of the other students. She had made friends
and was accepted by the upper-class British girls.

Back home once again, Ileana blossomed. Surrounded by her loving and
indulgent parents and her close friends, her liveliness and sense of humor
reasserted itself, the wounds from her year in school and Carol's betrayal
healed, and her warmth and charm rivaled her mother's.

During the fall, winter, and summer, she continued her schooling with
a tutor, as well as pursuing her nurse's training.

In the fall of 1926, seventeen-year-old Ileana was ecstatic to learn that she
and Nicky would be accompanying their mother on a tour of the United
States at Ferdinand's urging. They were worried about leaving him, as he
didn't look well, but he insisted he was only tired and they were not to
worry. His doctors concurred.

They departed in October of 1926 from Cherbourg, France, and were met with wild crowds when they docked in New York. They were treated to a ticker-tape parade and met at City Hall by Mayor Jimmy Walker, who escorted them to the train station, where they embarked for Washington, DC, to meet the president.

Ileana was shocked to discover that, unlike her own household and the households of the royalty she knew, presidents did not answer their own doors. No less than seven assistants were required to greet them and lead her, her mother, and Nicky to where President Coolidge waited. "I never saw so many in my life," she said later.

They took a train to the West Coast of the US, where Marie dedicated the Maryhill Museum, built and established by her friend, Col. Sam Hill. He, along with another American friend, dancer Loie Fuller, had come up with the idea for the tour. On the way home, the trip was marred for Ileana by a minor car accident, which confined her to bed for several days. Then, at Indianapolis, the news came that King Ferdinand was seriously ill, and they needed to get home at once.

Ileana was shocked at her father's appearance when she disembarked from the train in Bucharest. Thin to the point of emaciation, unsteady on his feet, and with a pallor that frightened her, he was obviously a very sick man. But he pushed her and everyone else's concern aside and turned the conversation to their trip, wanting all the details.

His insouciance was a bluff. Ferdinand had intestinal cancer. Marie was adamant that he not be told the true nature of his illness, and Ileana agreed. She promised to help make her father's last months comfortable and happy.

Soon after their return, Ferdinand underwent surgery, but he continued to sink until, by May, he essentially retired. First at Scroviste, just outside Bucharest, and then in Sinaia, Marie and Ileana sat with him in the tent erected on the lawns outside Marie's rooms, entertaining him with conversation and reading to him. He continued to weaken, and late at night on July 18, with Marie holding his hand, he died.

The morning after his death, Ileana was present as her six-year-old nephew, Prince Mihai, was proclaimed king, and his regency council, consisting of Ileana's brother, Prince Nicholas, Patriarch Miron Cristea, and Chief Justice George Buzdugan, was sworn in.

The day of the funeral, every building along the processional route in Bucharest was draped in black, and thousands of people turned out to pay their last respects to a king who had served them to the best of his ability and had considered them part of the family.

Thousands more Romanians lined the railway between Bucharest and Curtea de Arges. King Ferdinand was laid to rest in the tomb beside his uncle and aunt, with a thousand priests in attendance.

Ferdinand is a shadowy figure in Ileana's life. Her mother was a flamboyant and extroverted woman who drew the focus of a crowd, and whose charm and passion often eclipsed her shy, socially awkward husband. But he and Ileana were close in a quiet, behind-the-public-scenes way. Their shared tastes in reading and in fanciful play drew them together, and she always admired his devotion to duty.

༅༅༅ ༅༅༅ Ileana Remembers ༅༅༅ ༅༅༅

*H*e *and I were great admirers of Bulldog Drummond, and used to carry on long fanciful conversations, pretending we had met one or another of the characters in the series. . . .*

When I was about ten or twelve years old I developed a passion for dressing up, and I loved to arrange a costumed dinner party. My father joined in cheerfully when his duties permitted, and I remember one most successful evening when he put on an old dressing gown made of an Indian blanket which had been given him by the Red Cross during the war. Binding a few feathers around his head, he took the part of a red Indian chief to my entire satisfaction.

My father was at heart a quiet, gentle scholar, who all his life kept a lively interest in the science of botany. But above all else he was what the Germans call "pflichttreu," which means literally "duty-faithful." It was this innate sense of duty that made him overcome his personal shyness and gave him an air of royal dignity which made him stand out among other men, in spite of his retiring nature. One of his greatest personal pleasures was to go for long rambles with his dogs through the Sinaia forests, looking for rare plants for his rock garden. Deep satisfaction he also found among his books. I can see him now, his spectacles on his nose, one eye half shut because of the smoke of his cigar, one eyebrow a little raised, as with his beautifully shaped hands he selected a favorite volume, his long fingers lovingly turning the pages as he looked for a well-loved passage.

The whole nation wept as for the death of a dear parent. And with the unfailing perspicacity of the people they called him not "the Liberator"; not "the Victorious." For the title that should live in their hearts they gave him a dearer one: "Ferdinand the Loyal, King of the Peasants."

AS SHE RECOVERED FROM HER FATHER'S DEATH, Ileana's interests took her all over Romania and Europe as she traveled for her Guides and the Red Cross and to keep up with her wide and scattered family, including Carol, still living in Paris with Elena. But her anchor and the center of her world was Balcic, where her mother had retired after the first few weeks of widowhood.

Ileana visited Carol in 1928, when she was nineteen, the first family member to do so. As was her nature, she gave him the benefit of the doubt, forgave and forgot, and tried to restore the good relationship and feelings they'd shared for so many years. Carol, as grief-stricken as his sister, reciprocated and continued to insist that he wanted only the love of his family, and had no ambitions to return to Romania.

Carol was lying, at least in part. He did have ambitions that involved Romania—but he took care to conceal them from his sister. Ileana continued to believe in her brother and to encourage him through her visit and her letters.

Most of Ileana's time was taken up in her native country. She was still involved with the Romanian Red Cross and the YWCA Girl Reserves. She had made good on her vow to help establish the Romanian Guiding movement and had been active with them since 1925. In 1928, she was rewarded with her own troop of Guides. Thirty-two young women met with Ileana at the women's monastery in Horezu, a town south and west of Brasov, in the Oltania valley.

Queen Marie and Ileana in traditional Romanian dress

Here they worked for their merit badges and reveled

in the mountainous forests as they hiked and camped, sometimes for weeks at a time, under Ileana's gentle and sure leadership.

This period of Ileana's life, from the early 1920s to her marriage in 1931, deepened her love of her country and the people she counted not only as subjects, but as friends.

She was elected president of the YWCA reserves when she was in her late teens and spent a lot of time touring the country, giving speeches and representing the organization throughout Romania. In addition, as she wrote Carol in June of 1928, "With some money from a number of good people and with my own, I have built a marvelous house for the W.C.A. on a piece of land that Mother has given me. It can accommodate forty girls with all the modern facilities and it is also made in good taste."

She spent much of her leisure time at Balcic with her mother, where she painted and sculpted and worked on the gardens with Marie. Her interest in the sea and in sailing had grown over the years, and in Balcic she was free to indulge it, as she wrote to Carol in June of 1928:

"I, for one, am tremendously happy, since I have a small yacht, with an engine and sails as well, a twelve-tonner called *Isprava;** I spend all my time aboard her and it is like heaven to me. My passion for the sea keeps growing. All winter long, I have been studying navigation with Commander Pais, an excellent teacher and a most reliable man. Next spring, I intend to apply for a first-mate license."

She did this, she wrote later, because of her passion for the sea, but also because no one took her seriously until she passed the first-mate's license exams. They simply assumed that she was playing at being a sailor. Nothing could have been further from the truth. Ileana would have opted for a naval career, she told her mother, if her birth hadn't put that forever beyond her reach.

It was typical of Ileana that it never occurred to her that in the 1920s, women weren't naval officers— simply being a woman would have stopped her. And also typical of her, had she decided to do it, it's probable that she might have gone down in history as the

Ileana at Balcic, 1929

first woman officer of the Royal Romanian Navy. Ileana was never one to let convention stand in her way.

She passed her exams, and in the next years spent untold hours "steering her small vessel . . . among the waves. The sails offered themselves widely to the wind, like as many wings of large sea-gulls," wrote her mother, who watched from the balcony of Balcic.

It was here, Ileana always felt, that what she called her "arthritis" really began. She dived into the warm sea water for a swim after a day of sailing, but hit the wave the wrong way and was slammed against the yacht's side. Her crew, sailors from Romania's navy, quickly hauled her aboard and checked to make sure she was all right.

In truth, her spinal problems were probably a combination of the accident, the calcium and vitamin deficiencies she'd suffered in the war, and the scoliosis she'd had since birth.

Twenty years old in 1929, Ileana stood on the brink of a new decade and adulthood, facing a happy and fruitful maturity. Like all lives, however, her future contained both sorrow and joy—both of which would be found sometimes at the least expected times and in the most surprising places.

CHAPTER NINE

Love & Marriage

Take wives and beget sons and daughters; and take wives for your sons,
and give your daughters to husbands; and be multiplied and not diminished.
(Jeremiah 36:6)

By 1929, Ileana had matured into a beautiful and graceful woman. She had the "most perfect" figure in Romania, according to the director of the National Physical Academy. She reveled in tennis and skiing, as well as the sailing, swimming, and riding she'd loved for years. The activity kept her fit and slim. She carried her five-foot-ten-inch frame with a dancer's grace. Her blue-grey eyes dominated her oval face and shapely head.

It wasn't only the director of the academy who noticed her figure or her engaging and warm personality. She was a popular young woman, twenty years of age now, whose name was linked with those of some of the most eligible bachelors in Europe, among them the prince of Wales and the king of Bulgaria. But Ileana was not one to keep a string of men. For her, love was serious business, and she wasn't going to give her heart lightly. She dated many, including the Infante Don Alfonso of Spain, Prince of Asturias, heir to the Spanish throne. She met him during a visit to her Aunty Bee, Marie's sister, in Spain in 1929. The hemophiliac prince fell in love with her at once and quickly proposed. Ileana, whose heart was tender and who had been raised to succor and care for the disadvantaged, was inclined to accept. Marie, warned by her sister about the prince's lecherous father, convinced Ileana she would be making a mistake.

On her twenty-first birthday, Ileana's mother threw a costume party for her. Ileana was taken with the blonde good looks, blue eyes rimmed with black eyelashes, and the brilliant smile of one of the guests. The son of Marie's good friend, Daisy Pless, Alexander (or Lexel) of Pless was equally smitten with Ileana. The two were quickly inseparable, and in early February, announced their engagement and a June wedding date.

In late February, however, the Romanian government unexpectedly canceled the engagement. Unknown to Ileana, Lexel had been accused of engaging in a homosexual encounter when he was eighteen. While nothing was ever proven, simply the knowledge of the accusation would be a scandal if it got out. Shortly after the official announcement, though, a palace aide leaked the reason to the press.

Ileana was heartbroken. Truly and deeply in love, she was in no shape to face the storm of controversy the news generated. Even publications as respected as *Time* Magazine reported not only the breakup of the engagement, but the reason for it. To shield Ileana from the press and the avid public, Marie took her to Egypt.

But even there, heartbreak followed. Lexel, equally devastated at the news, followed Ileana. Enlisting the help of a dear friend, he wrote a love note declaring his devotion and begging Ileana to reconsider her decision, and concealed it in a bouquet which his friend presented to the princess when they "accidentally" met in Alexandria. But the decision was not up to Ileana—the government had forced the break, and she had to succumb to her duty.

But Ileana's troubles were not all personal. In June, with both Ileana and Marie out of the country, Carol landed in Bucharest and proceeded to take over the government. He announced to his brother Nicky and the prime minister, who had negotiated his return, that contrary to the agreement he had made with them, he would not simply act as regent for his now nine-year-old son. He would take the throne himself.

Imagine This

"What I do as king is my own business, Ileana. Don't tell me how to rule my country."

Ileana stands by Carol's desk, fists clenched and lips set in a tight line. She inhales deeply, hoping to calm herself enough to answer him rationally, instead of screaming at him as she longs to do. "I'm not telling you how to run the country. But I can't stand by and say nothing.

"You're treating Mother and Sitta terribly! The things you've said about your ex-wife are horrible! And she's the mother of the heir to your throne, she's the first lady of the country, so why take her portrait away from the public? Why blacken her name so badly?"

"And what's she done to me? She's blackened my name far more than I have hers—she's made me out to be a playboy, a psychopath, a cruel and heartless, philandering husband, a socialist who's less interested in the throne than in the power that comes with it. I'm not to punish her for this disloyalty?" Carol looks over at Ileana, amazement on his face. "And you would side with her against your own brother? After all the years we've shared? After all the years of closeness?"

Ileana waves her hand, dismissing his accusation. "It's that closeness that pushes me to speak now! I know what you're capable of, I know what you can do and be when you set your mind to it. But you aren't doing that, you're hurting the people who love you most, who want the best for you, and who want you to be a king the way our father was, Carol.

"And you know it's you who've brought this harvest. Sitta says nothing about you in public. Not now and not before the divorce. It's your own actions that have given you the reputation you have. And that doesn't excuse your treatment of Mother, either. Taking all her money away, surrounding her with spies and traitors, isolating her from Barbu— you know how much she relies on him! She's always supported you, always encouraged—"

"Oh, yes, Mother encouraged me. She really encouraged me, Ileana, when she said I was less than a man. She forced me to give up Zizi. She made me disavow my son, Mircea. She really 'encouraged' me, didn't she? She's always hated me, she's always wanted to make me into something I'm not, and this is her harvest for all the years she mistreated me."

Ileana whirls away and paces to the window. "What you're doing is wrong, it's cowardly, and it's dishonorable."

"Dishonorable!" Carol's voice, already loud, rises even more as he loses his temper completely. He strides across the room and takes Ileana by the arms, shaking her in his fury. "You dare to call the king dishonorable? I'll show you." He lets her go so quickly she staggers as he continues to yell. "You think you can come here and upbraid your king? Get out of my sight—get out! I won't have you or anyone telling me how to rule, telling me what is dishonorable or honorable. Quit the Girl Guides— I, your king, demand it. And I'm removing you as the head of the YWCA reserves, too, and I forbid you to visit the officers in your regiment. Now get out of my sight, you pious, dried-up old maid!"

Ileana stumbles to the door, wrenches it open and flees down the hall, Carol's insults and venom following her until she reaches her apartments and slams the door, weeping in fear and sorrow.

THE FINAL STRAW CAME LATER THAT AUGUST, when Ileana learned that Carol's lover, Elena Lupescu, had returned to Romania and was secreted in the palace.

To escape the ever-increasing pressure and isolation, Ileana traveled to Germany in March of 1931 to visit her father's family. While there, she became reacquainted with Archduke Anton of the House of Habsburg. Anton wasn't there by accident or coincidence. Carol had asked their German relatives to invite him, hoping that Anton and Ileana would be attracted to each other and marry. If they did, Ileana would likely live outside Romania, leaving more of the public's attention to be focused on Carol.

Ileana had met Anton in 1929, during her visit to Aunty Bee in Spain. His father was the nephew of the late Austrian emperor Franz Joseph, and his mother was a Spanish Bourbon, with an ancestry nearly as illustrious as Ileana's.

Although royal, Anton and his family were *heimatlos** or stateless. They had been exiled from Austria in 1918 when the country became a republic, and their citizenship, lands, and income had been stripped from them. Educated as an engineer and a pilot, Anton had been working at a gas station when they met, and flying airplanes as a barnstormer for fun and to earn extra money.

On this encounter in Germany, Ileana did not have the ardent and invalid Spanish prince to distract her, and as she later recalled, they "found there were many things we had in common. We liked flying and we got on very well."

So well, in fact, that on April 20, 1931, Ileana wrote to Carol, "I feel I have really found the man who will make me happy. Of course, the future lies in the hands of God, but, since I trust Him, I think that Anton is the one with whom I will be able and confident to face life, that I will find in him the partner and support I so much need." Carol happily consented to the engagement, and the wedding was set for July.

In late June, Ileana met with Monsignor Vladimir Ghika, an official of the Roman Catholic Church, who informed her that the pope had declined her request to be allowed to marry with both Catholic and Orthodox rites. "I have been deeply upset by the news," she wrote Carol. "It is through her [the Church] that I have always perceived the spirit of my Romanian Land. My soul hurts when I think of leaving . . . without the blessing of the Church in which I have been baptized, brought up and taught to express myself."

Through Prince Ghika, Carol suggested that instead, she should receive the Holy Eucharist the morning before the wedding. She agreed, but asked that he be with her for the Liturgy. The shared Eucharist was the last time Ileana saw her brother with affection or love.

July 24, 1931, dawned cloudy and threatening with rain, but it was sunny and bright in the Grand Hall of Peles Castle at Sinaia, where Ileana and Anton were married in a civil wedding.

She wore a long embroidered white silk dress that outlined her figure, with a long sweeping train. It had a soft V-neck with a small shawl collar. Her veil was white tulle, over which the traditional Romanian *beteala** were twisted, to fall over her shoulders like a shower of gold.

The wedding and reception were the most magnificent the royal family had ever experienced, and the gifts were equally magnificent. But Ileana's dearest, most cherished wedding present came from Marie. Among the jewels Uncle Joe had brought back from Russia in 1918 was a diamond and sapphire tiara that Ileana's mother had inherited from her mother, Marie Alexandrovna. The tiara had been made for Ileana's great-great-grandmother, Princess Charlotte of Prussia, and given to her by her husband, Tsar Nicholas I, in 1825. The tiara resembled a crown more than anything else. It was set with diamonds and sapphires nearly the size of a man's pocket watch.

The day after the civil ceremony, a gala dinner with 600 guests was held at Peles Castle. The next day, July 26, Ileana and Anton were married by Archbishop Alexandru Cisar and Monsignor Vladimir Ghika in the Catholic ceremony.

Section III

Marriage & War

Archduke Anton and Archduchess Ileana with their six children. Top: Magi, Stefan, Herzi. Bottom: Dominic, Sandi, Minola.

TIMELINE 1931–1943

YEAR	COUNTRY	EVENT
1931	Romania	Ileana marries Archduke Anton Habsburg, effectively exiled from Romania by Carol
	Germany	Four million unemployed people
1932	Austria	Ileana and Anton's first child, Stefan Habsburg, born; they move to Sonnberg Castle
1933	Austria	Ileana and Anton's second child, Maria Ileana (Minola), born
	Germany	Adolf Hitler becomes chancellor of Germany
1934	Germany	Hitler becomes permanent dictator
1935	Austria	Ileana and Anton's second daughter, Alexandra (Sandi), born
1936	Austria	Queen Marie's last visit to Sonnberg—Ileana notices her illness
	Britain	King George V dies; Edward VII succeeds him; Edward VII abdicates, succeeded by Prince Albert, known as King George VI
	USA	F. D. Roosevelt re-elected president
	Spain	Spanish Civil War begins
	Germany	Occupies demilitarized Rhineland
1937	Austria	Ileana and Anton's son Dominic (Niki) born
	Britain	Neville Chamberlain becomes prime minister
	USA	Hindenburg disaster; Amelia Earhart disappears on trans-Pacific flight
	Germany-Italy	Italy joins Comintern Pact
1938	Austria	Ileana and Anton's third daughter, Maria Magdalena (Magi), born
	Romania	Carol becomes dictator of Romania; death of Queen Marie
	Austria	Anschluss—invasion of Austria by Germany
	Germany	"Night of Glass"— beginning of the Holocaust; Sudetenland crisis
	Austria	Anton Habsburg volunteers for German air force
	Britain	Neville Chamberlain signs the "Munich Agreement"

YEAR	COUNTRY	EVENT
1939	Germany	Invades Poland
	Britain/Canada	Declare war on Germany after Polish invasion
	USA	Remains neutral
	USSR	Invades Finland
1940	Romania	Hitler carves up Romania—Bessarabia to USSR, Transylvania to Hungary, the Southern Dobrudja to Bulgaria; Carol forced to abdicate, Mihai set up as puppet king by Ion Antonescu
	Britain	Neville Chamberlain resigns, Winston Churchill becomes prime minister
	Western Europe	Fall of Netherlands, Belgium, and France (including Dunkirk evacuation); Battle of Britain—July to October; ends with Germany repulsed
	Germany/ Poland	Auschwitz Death Camp opens
1941	Romania	Allies with Nazi Germany
	USSR, Germany, Romania	Launch of Russian invasion by Germany, supported by Romania; Battle of Moscow; Siege of Leningrad
	USA	Japanese attack on Pearl Harbor, entry of USA into WWII
1942	Austria	Ileana and Anton's fourth daughter, Elizabeth (Herzi), born
	Austria	Ileana begins nursing Romanian wounded from Eastern Front battles; appointed officially by Romanian Govt. to minister to Romanian wounded in the Reich
	Pacific	Singapore falls; Philippines surrender; Battle of Midway; Battle of Guadalcanal
	Europe	Dieppe Raid
	Pacific	Invasion of Aleutian Islands by Japan
1943	Austria	Small hospital established at Sonnberg for Romanian wounded
	Europe	Tripoli captured by British forces; Battle of Stalingrad ends; Siege of Leningrad ends; surrender of German & Italian forces in N. Africa; Allied invasion & surrender of Italy; Battle of Kursk
	Pacific	Defense of Aleutian Islands by USA

CHAPTER TEN

Joy & Sorrow

How shall we sing the Lord's song
In a foreign land?
(Psalm 136:4)

Imagine This

Ileana stares at her brother Carol in shock. "You can't be serious," she gasps, falling back into the chair behind her.

Carol nods. "I'm very sorry, but it must be this way. You understand—this is duty, and politics, Ileana. You of all people understand duty, surely."

"But not to live here? This is my home! I've lived in Romania all my life, I am Romanian."

Ileana gropes beside her and grips Anton's hand. How could she live anywhere else, she thinks. This is home—this is her place. Her head whirls in shock as she glances at Anton, who looks equally baffled.

"Carol, why?" she asks with a catch in her voice. "This country is my home, the people are as much my family as Mama and you! How will I live without my people?" She turns away, stifling a sob.

"It's too tedious to go into detail," Carol says. "The political situation here is unstable. Mihai's regency council was useless, and they've left the country in a mess. Having Anton living here, especially if you live in Transylvania, as you've talked about, would be disastrous."

"I don't understand," says Anton. He squeezes Ileana's hand tightly. "What do I have to do with the regency council and the mess they left?"

"No offense to you, Anton. But you're a Habsburg. The Habsburgs—" Carol throws his hands in the air, letting them slap his thighs for emphasis. "What can I say without offending you? I can't, so let me be blunt, and forgive any hurt I cause. Transylvania was ground under the Austrian heel for so long, they were so badly treated, and to them the Habsburgs *are* Austria. The Romanian people who live in Transylvania would not put up with a Habsburg living there, married to their favorite daughter. I'm sorry—it's not up to me, really. If it were, I'd give you a place of your own myself. This on top of everything else could bring down the government."

Ileana marshals all her strength, and she and Anton try to persuade Carol to change his mind, but nothing sways him—they may not live in Romania, and that is all there is to it. All their arguments are met with the same implacable reasons—Anton's presence would foment at the least a fall of government and at the worst, revolution.

"But where will we go?" Ileana asks finally. "We had planned to live here, we were going to stay at Bran—now what will we do?"

"But I'm not demanding you leave immediately!" Carol cries. He pats his sister on the shoulder. "I'm not an ogre. You don't have to pack up and leave this minute, I can be more generous than that. You hurt me, little sister, thinking I'd just throw you out like a beggar! We're family, I can be generous with family."

Ileana, too shocked, hurt, and angry to listen anymore, tugs on Anton's hand. He nods, they bow and leave.

WHILE THE POLITICAL SITUATION WAS UNSTABLE, Anton's family connections weren't the problem Carol made them seem. This was more of Carol's plan to isolate Ileana from both her country and her mother. He had even instructed the Romanian embassies and legations in Germany and Austria not to welcome Ileana and Anton or extend them any courtesies (although he didn't tell Ileana that).

Carol was acting out of jealousy. Both Marie and Ileana were immensely popular in Romania, beloved by everyone from the highest *voivod** to the lowliest peasant. In spite of the fact that Carol's return was greeted with crowds whose size had not been seen since his parents' return from Jassy at the end of World War I, in spite of the fact that he was given a fifteen-minute ovation on his first speech as king, Carol didn't want to share the limelight. No one could be as popular as himself, so he took steps to ensure no one was. By denying Ileana and Anton permission to live in Romania, he not only kept the people's attention on himself, he also interfered with Ileana's relationship with their mother and isolated them from each other's support.

Ileana couldn't refuse him—he was the king of Romania and she was his subject. But it was the breaking point in her relations with her brother. She continued to write to him, she was polite and fulfilled the obligations a sister owes a brother and a subject owes her monarch, but never again did she trust or confide in him as she had done in the past.

As with everything else in her life, Ileana made the best of the situation, and she was deeply in love with Anton. That alone was a source of deep and lasting joy. She had her faith—while she had married in the Catholic Church, she continued to live an Orthodox life.

They honeymooned at Bran Castle, and in September left for Munich, where they'd rented a house from Aunty Bee. Ileana delighted in furnishing and setting up her new home:

"I can now say I have a home," she wrote to a friend, Natalia Slivici, in October of 1931, "except for a couple of lamps and some other details. It is so terribly cozy, I feel so good in it . . . since it is so full of love and happiness. I wouldn't have thought it possible to feel so content."

By spring, Ileana was expecting. Her pregnancy wasn't easy, and she was ill for a great deal of the time, but she was deeply happy about it nevertheless. In the summer of 1932, less than a year after they'd moved to Munich, Anton obtained permission to return to Austria, although he was still denied citizenship. They found and leased a house in Mödling, just south of Vienna.

Ileana's dearest wish was to return to Romania to give birth to her first child, which was due in August, but Carol's response was evident in a letter Ileana wrote in July to her old and dear friend, Mrs. Tasca:

"It is with deep sorrow and grief that I am writing to you. The Government have apparently decided that it would prove a danger for the State and for their chances in the elections if I came to give birth in my own country, so *my Country's gates are sealed for me as they would be for an enemy and I have to remain among strangers.* . . . It is so ugly, so utterly ugly, and it hurts, it hurts to the bottom of my heart and I do not know how to cope with such a disgrace" (Ileana's emphasis).

That wasn't the only insult "the government"—and since Carol was virtual dictator, that meant Carol—threw her way. That year was also the fifth anniversary of their father's death, and Ileana longed to return to participate in the memorial. She wrote Carol for permission, but he was adamant. She could not return for the commemoration of their father's repose, she could not return to have her baby, she could not return, she could not return, she could not return.

By August, when the baby was due, Ileana had accepted the situation and come up with an alternative plan. Her mother would travel to Mödling to be with Ileana for the birth. She brought with her a pottery box filled with dirt from Romania. Ileana went into labor on the twelfth of August, and Marie slipped the box under Ileana's bed. But her labor was

Ileana with Anton and baby Stefan

difficult and prolonged, and it was three days before Stefan Habsburg, Archduke of Austria, was born "on Romanian soil."

Ileana's joy at her first son's birth was enhanced not only by her mother's presence, but by the fact that word of Carol's cruelty had leaked out. In an effort to make up for her heartbreak, Austria greeted the new archduke with cannon salutes and church bells, in spite of the fact that, like his father, Stefan was officially *heimatlos*.

Carol, when news of the Austrian reception reached him, was shamed into inviting his sister into Romania for a few weeks.

Stefan was joined by a sister, also stateless, the following December. Marie Ileana, whom they called Minola, was born with the pot of Romanian soil under the bed on December 18, 1932.

Like all young parents, Ileana and Anton wanted their own house in the country so their children could run and play safely. In 1934, they bought a rundown, trash-filled, broken-up old castle and eighteen acres of land about thirty miles north of Vienna, in Sonnberg.

The castle was a fairy-tale-like building. Ileana's sister-in-law described it best: "In the centre there is a well; around the well stands the castle; around the castle is an island; around the island is a moat; around the moat is a park; and around the park runs a river."

Anton supervised the renovation, and his inventive solutions often showed the workmen a way to accomplish what he and Ileana wanted after his contractors had said something couldn't be done.

The family moved in before renovations were completed, conducting the traditional house blessing amid half-cleared rooms, electrical wires, and plaster dust.

CHAPTER ELEVEN

Family Life

Your wife shall be like a vine, prospering on the sides of your house;
Your children like newly planted olive trees around your table.
(Psalm 127:3)

nce again, Ileana refused to live as a stereotypical archduchess, as she was now styled. While she did hire a cook, maids, and laundresses from the small village of Sonnberg, it was only to protect her family and staff from her own incompetence and ignorance.

Growing up as a princess meant that the time she'd spent giving speeches, running the youth organizations, and training as a nurse meant she hadn't learned the homey, traditional jobs that most of us take for granted. "It would have been egotism on my part to take time that belonged to the country in order to learn to do things that were being done well and efficiently by others," is the way she put it.

Much of the family's food was produced on their land, and Ileana dove into the life of a farmwife with zest and enthusiasm. She supervised the beehives, learned to shear the sheep, negotiated the lease of some of her land to local farmers, and raised cash crops of potatoes, wheat, and corn. She spun the wool she'd sheared and knitted it into socks and sweaters for her family. She sewed and planned decorative art projects for the castle.

While prevented from returning to Romania as often as she wished, or for the birth of her next child, Alexandra (Sandi), in December of 1935 (also born "on Romanian soil"), she didn't lack for her mother's company. Marie visited Sonnberg so often they put aside a suite of rooms for her.

The village became for Ileana something of a substitute for her lost country and a way to continue doing the charitable work she loved. She opened a small dispensary for the village and established a troop of Girl Guides. She opened a canteen for the poor in a ground-floor room of the castle and hired an old woman to cook. Following in her mother's footsteps, she enlisted her own children to help as soon as they could carry a tray and toddle.

The villagers and staff joined the family for skating parties, feasts, and Christmas celebrations. Anton, one of his brothers, or another male guest would play the part of Saint Nicholas, handing out the candy and tiny gifts that Ileana had prepared and wrapped.

Visits to and from Anton's nine brothers and sisters were frequent, especially during holidays, and the castle was more often than not filled with visitors, friends, family, and staff, all busy but ready to drop everything for a moment's play or laughter.

During the summers, the family flew in Anton's homemade plane to Lake Wörthsee, in Southern Germany, for their annual vacation. As Anton was a licensed pilot, it wasn't hard to fly from there across the mountains to visit Mignon, Queen of Yugoslavia, or to Britain, or Germany, or Spain, to visit other relatives on both sides of the family.

But the highlights of Ileana's years in Sonnberg were, without doubt, her mother's visits. As close to her mother as ever, and worried about her under Carol's unceasing persecution, Ileana as well as everyone else looked forward to Marie's trips.

But Marie worried in turn about her daughter. She fretted about how hard it was for Ileana to carry children and give birth, and wondered if she was wasting her life. But her daughter reassured her—"Mama, I'm climbing a staircase, and now I'm sitting on the landing." Her time to shine was not yet, she felt, but it would come.

Through it all, Ileana kept her faith—the castle had been blessed according to Orthodox tradition, and she prayed regularly in her icon corner. Sometimes she'd sit in the gardens, dreaming of "building a monastery in a glorious place in the mountains to later retire to." However, she raised the children, as she'd promised, as Catholics.

Christmas 1936 was one of the best holidays Ileana ever remembered. Marie was there and had crocheted small caps for the village children. They skated on the river and the moat with the children—Stefan, four and a half, Minola, three, and baby Sandi, nineteen months old, all bundled up. St. Nicholas visited, as usual, and the days seemed tinged with a special blessing. Perhaps it was simply that it was the last truly carefree time in Ileana's life, unshadowed by terror, war, or exile.

That holiday, although joyous, was also stressful. She was expecting her fourth child and took pains to conceal the fact from Marie. For someone as usually observant as Marie, that would have been difficult, for Ileana was ill through all of her pregnancies and had great difficulties delivering her children. But Marie wasn't herself, either. Ileana noted that she looked tired and unwell.

At the time, Ileana put it down to the grief her mother had suffered that last year—among others, she'd lost her beloved sister Ducky, and living under Carol's harsh and unceasing scrutiny was a constant strain.

But Ileana's worry was justified. By March, Marie was seriously ill. The doctors eventually determined that she was suffering from cirrhosis of the liver. But that was ridiculous, Ileana thought—how could she have contracted an alcoholic's disease when she never touched alcohol? Today we know of several conditions that can cause cirrhosis in people who don't drink, but diagnostics weren't as advanced in the 1930s, so the origin of Marie's cirrhosis remained a mystery that will never be solved.

Ileana was doubly disappointed, for when Dominic (Niki) was born in the summer of 1937, she still wasn't allowed to return to Romania for the birth, and her mother wasn't well enough to come to see her. Her joy in Niki, however, reconciled her, and she talked with her mother on the phone.

Over the next months, Marie rallied a few times, but her condition worsened until finally Carol agreed to transfer her to a sanitarium in Italy. In 1938, Ileana visited Marie, leaving Anton and the children at home for a few days, and was deeply concerned at the lack of diagnosis and treatment.

On the morning of March 12, she and Marie were listening to the radio when they were paralyzed by the news that Hitler's forces had just marched into Austria. Ileana was frantic, consumed with the need to return and protect her children.

CHAPTER TWELVE

Death & Destruction

The source of life is laid in the tomb,
and the tomb itself becomes a ladder to heaven.
(Dormition Vespers)

arie completely understood. She immediately sent a cable to alert Anton and ordered her car to take Ileana to the station, where she boarded the next train for Vienna.

The trip back, once they were across the Austrian border, was a fore-taste of the next years of Ileana's life under the Nazi regime.

Imagine This

The train had stopped. Again. Normally it took almost all day to reach Vienna from the border, but at this rate, with the disorganization and the crowds and uncertainty, they'd be lucky to get there in three days! Things were barely moving, with no one sure of just what the Anschluss* would mean. At the head of the car, Ileana noticed the conductor talking heatedly with some people, moving backward as a group of young men and women forced their way on board.

"We are Hitler's loyalty investigators," they announced. "We will question those of you we choose to—the conductor will show us your passports. If we think you are not loyal to Hitler, the Reich,* and the glorious liberation of Austria, well, so much the worse for you. We will convince you, be sure of it!"

The conductor, a small, fatherly-looking man with a mustache and graying temples, scurried ahead, gathering the passports and glancing quickly at them. He noted Ileana's, issued by the Austrian government in her married name—the Archduchess of Habsburg. He slid it into the growing pile and gave her a sympathetic look and a pat on the shoulder.

Her hands grew clammy. How could she handle these young thugs and hoodlums? They'd be sure to target her as an enemy of the Reich, simply because of her name.

They moved slowly down the car, demanding passports and calling out the names of those the conductor handed them. One man, a businessman from the look of his suit and his well-groomed hair, refused to answer their more personal questions. They hauled him from his seat and shoved him off the train, and Ileana could hear low thuds and his cries as some of the thugs hustled him away.

Finally they left—without ever having questioned Ileana. She relaxed into her seat as the train slowly gathered speed. The conductor handed back her documents and smiled reassuringly. Somehow he'd managed to conceal hers in the pile, and they'd never known that the Archduchess of Habsburg was on the train.

Grateful to him, but unable to express her thanks for fear of being overheard, she sat quiet and anxious until the train pulled into the station at Vienna.

ANTON GREETED HER, and she had another shock when they returned to the car. It was draped in a Nazi flag. Horrified, Ileana demanded that Anton remove it. He explained that no car was allowed to move without it, and unwillingly Ileana climbed in for the ride back to Sonnberg. On the way, Anton told her of their experience.

On March 12, fifty *Sturmabteilung*,* or storm troopers, had arrived at the castle, suspicious and on edge. It had taken all of Anton's tact to keep them from acting stupidly, and he confessed that there had been times when he was afraid things might have exploded into violence. When Marie's cable had arrived, they suspected Anton might be plotting an escape. He had needed to exercise all his charm to convince them that his wife was *arriving* in Vienna, not escaping! Finally realizing they had the children as hostages, they allowed him to meet Ileana.

The troops stayed with the family for the next ten days. The "storm troopers," Ileana realized, were nothing more than punks and bullies from the neighboring villages, including Sonnberg itself.

For the first month of the occupation, Ileana and her family were subjected to frequent and unexpected house searches from the storm troopers and the Gestapo.* Simply being Habsburg and royal was reason enough for the family to be harassed. They learned to answer questions politely and do exactly as they were told. They made no sudden movements, not even to save a delicate object as the soldiers swept tables and chests clear to check for hiding spots. Their papers were examined, letters read, and finances scrutinized. Sending money abroad or even receiving letters that criticized the government was (or could be interpreted as) traitorous.

Finally, the family was told there would be no more searches, but soldiers would be billeted* with them.

As the new order took shape, Ileana's thoughts focused again on her mother. Marie was moved to a clinic in Dresden in mid-May, but her physician told Ileana there was nothing the doctors could do for her. Marie would be more comfortable at home.

Marie returned to Romania in July. Brokenhearted, worried, and still unsettled with conditions in Austria, Ileana and Anton postponed their annual summer vacation at Wörthsee.

Ileana Remembers

It was on July 18, 1938, that I received a telephone call telling me my mother was dying. Here the difficulties of the political situation in Austria, which had been a constant undercurrent of worry through all my concern for my mother, met us in full force. You can imagine receiving such a message; perhaps you have at some time received exactly that same message; but in the United States you cannot imagine being unable to respond to it—yet that was my situation. . . . The new German passports had not yet been issued. Not only were we unable to leave the new "Reich" without a passport, but it would be hopeless to attempt to cross the Hungarian frontier and travel across Hungary without one. It was with the power of desperation that I started the wheels moving. I still remember the last frantic mishap. The Hungarian Consulate in Vienna had been notified that we would be coming for visas on our new passports, and they were kindness itself about agreeing to wait. Inside the Consulate sat an officer ready to give us our visas—but at the door of the Consulate stood a porter who had not been notified of our arrival, and he refused to let us in.

"The Consulate is closed!" he announced firmly, and shut the door in our faces.

When he closed the door in my face, I felt for a moment that insanity of despair which is the special cross of the oppressed and the downtrodden. Then, rallying my forces, I pressed the doorbell again, keeping my finger on it until the porter in a towering rage opened the door a crack to threaten me. Throwing myself against it, I thrust my foot and my arm into the crack, and said with passionate determination, "But I shall go in!" And on this wave of determination I was indeed inside, with neither the porter nor I knowing exactly why he had given way, and in a short time I had the Hungarian visas.

Anton and I set out in the car for a nineteen-hour drive across Austria, Hungary, and Romania. In the very early morning we came to the Romanian frontier, and I asked the guards if they had any word from the palace, but they said no—no word. When I returned to Austria ten days later they begged my forgiveness. "But we could not bear to be the ones to tell you of the Queen's death, Domnitza!"* they said.

Yet on that first morning I think I knew in my heart what had happened, even though I refused to acknowledge it to myself until we came to the town of Cluj after sunrise and saw the flags all flying at half-mast. My mother had died at five o'clock the day before—while I was still desperately struggling for permission to come to her.

IN ONE BLOW, ILEANA HAD LOST HER BEST FRIEND, her mother, and her queen. Even though she knew it was coming, she was left with an emptiness that nothing could fill. "It is a terrible thing to be nobody's child," she thought. It was something her mother had said years ago, and now Ileana understood it.

It helped that Carol gave his mother a full state funeral, and the Romanian public responded with an outpouring of their love for the woman they'd called "Mother."

Her body lay in state for three days at Cotroceni, the coffin heaped with red flowers. After the funeral liturgy it was borne through the streets of Bucharest to the train station. Over 250,000 people lined the streets along the route, under the mauve banners Marie had wished for.

Normally a two-hour trip, the train took six hours to reach Curtea de Arges, delayed while the people of Romania said their last goodbyes to their beloved queen. Hundreds of thousands of people knelt by the tracks, holding lighted candles and throwing flowers on the open carriage that held her coffin. So many flowers were thrown that her honor guard, who surrounded her casket on the flat car, were in danger of being suffocated.

In the days and weeks following her mother's burial, Ileana discovered again just how much she and her mother had loved each other. In her will, Marie confirmed Ileana's ownership of the sapphire and diamond tiara and left her Bran Castle, the W.C.A. land and buildings at Balcic she'd given Ileana, as well as a house in Bucharest. In addition, she left a full quarter of her money to Ileana, with the remaining three-quarters to be distributed between Carol, Mignon, Lisabeta, and Nicky.

CHAPTER THIRTEEN

War Wife

Those who sow with tears
Shall reap with exceeding joy.
(Psalm 125:5)

leana adjusted to life without her mother and with the increasing restrictions and tension that life in the German Reich brought with it. It became apparent that universal conscription was inevitable, and they decided that Anton would volunteer for the Luftwaffe* rather than being drafted into the army.

On August 31, 1939, Hitler invaded Poland, which was the trigger for World War II, as Britain, quickly followed by other nations, declared war.

Like many women during any war, Ileana had to adjust to life as a single mother. But it wasn't just her immediate family for whom she was responsible. She had the castle staff to look after and villagers who depended on her for nursing, morale, and food.

Ileana was expected to supply the soldiers she billeted with linen and blankets, rooms, beds and other necessary furniture, and provide living quarters (officers were housed in the castle, while the men stayed in the village). She was never informed in advance of their arrival or how long they'd stay. They might number anywhere from ten to fifty and stay for anywhere from three days to six weeks.

In addition to accommodating the soldiers, Ileana, along with the rest

of Austria, had to adjust to life during war. Fuel rationing was a problem—
the castle had thirty-five rooms, and heating them used a lot of oil or coal.
To save gas, everyone rode bicycles or horses or walked, unless the distance
or importance of the errand justified the use of a car.

Food rationing was in effect, and farm production was checked. Quotas
were established not only for the amount, but for the type of food to be
produced. While adhering to the rules, Ileana still managed to order items
from Romania for treats on special occasions, like candy for Christmas,
extra sugar, special cheeses, and bottles of sherbet.

Clothing was rationed. No one was allowed more than two pairs of shoes.
The family, with four active, growing children, learned to pass things down,
darn, patch, and mend. Ileana came up with creative measures for making
clothes—at one point, she and the girls wore reworked curtains.

With universal conscription a reality, most of the able-bodied men in the
area were gone, which left the women responsible for both their own and
the men's work. The responsibilities weighed heavily on all of them, but

Ileana and her daughters in their dresses made from curtains

more so on Ileana. The entire responsibility for the estate and the household lay solely on her shoulders.

Maria Magdalena, or Magi, Ileana's fifth child, was born on the second of October, 1939. Her father didn't hear of her birth until several days afterward, stationed as he was in France as an air courier.

Once she had weaned the baby, Ileana took nursing courses from the German Red Cross while continuing to shoulder the burdens imposed by the war and the Nazi regime.

Since all news and communication were state-controlled, it was almost impossible to determine the fate of her friends and family in the rest of Europe or the true course of the war. Marvelous victories were touted, some of which, like the fall of France in 1940, were true, and there weren't a lot of losses to report—Germany was winning as they marched through the Netherlands, Belgium, France, and nations to the east of Germany, and all the Reich knew it.

As they adjusted to the irregularities of wartime, Ileana realized that the rhythm of her life was keyed to Anton's leave schedule. When he could, he would come home, and for a week or two the entire household would rejoice and relax, seizing any opportunities for enjoyment "with exaggerated gratitude because they allowed us . . . for a moment . . . to forget the horrors of war."

In the summer of 1940, Anton was granted a longer than usual furlough, probably because he was being transferred from courier duty in France, after its surrender, to flying instruction near Berlin. The family managed a brief vacation in Wörthsee, where they hiked and swam and where Ileana began teaching Stefan to sail.

Anton's visits were few and far between. Most of the time, the leaves were only a few hours or a couple of days long, not enough to travel to Sonnberg to see the family. When she was able to, Ileana would take the train to wherever he was stationed.

While visiting Anton in Berlin in the late fall or early winter of 1940, she stayed for a few days while ill at the Romanian Legation. Because of the restriction of news, she knew almost nothing of events in her homeland, and the minister, while glad to see his princess, had the misfortune to bring her sorrowful tidings.

Romania had again chosen neutrality when the war broke out, for the same reasons as before. But in the summer of 1940, the Soviet Union had invaded Bessarabia, while Germany handed Hungary the northern part of Transylvania, and at the same time presented to Bulgaria the southern Dobrudja (which included Marie's old estate at Balcic). The fact that Hitler simply chopped the country up and handed it out to his allies, without a word of protest from the king, destroyed Carol's power, and Ion Antonescu, Ileana's old friend and the prime minister, forced the king's abdication just weeks before Ileana's visit to Berlin.

Carol and Elena Lupescu fled Romania. Mihai, Carol's twenty-year-old son, was installed as king. In early October, over 500,000 Nazi troops began crossing into Romania. By November, Romania had joined the Axis in the war.

Ileana was torn over the news. Although she ached for her country's troubles and for the mess Carol had made of both his life and his reign, his abdication and flight meant she was free, if she chose, to return home anytime she wanted, for however long she wanted. Likewise, with Romania on the side of the Nazis, travel to Romania was much simpler. But she was no fan of the fascist state and grieved for Ion's choice.

For the time being, the news was something she carried in her heart. With most of the able-bodied men at the front, the women were still trying to cope with the double duties they'd had to assume, and Ileana was badly needed at Sonnberg. The military billetings were especially stressful because they continued with no warning or predictability, and the staff didn't cope well with the men.

The soldiers' personalities varied enormously—some were pleasant and helpful, others fanatic Nazis. Some were educated and polite, while still others were rude and boorish. Ileana was needed to smooth whatever rough edges and conflicts arose, although she found it as frustrating as did everyone else.

No matter how she disagreed with their policies or disliked their personalities, Ileana always treated the soldiers as honored guests. Even when they acted like thugs and bullies, she maintained a calm and polite demeanor. But occasionally, she was able to exact a sweet revenge.

The current billeting is small, and the men polite and good-natured—so much so that Ileana decides to ask them to have lunch with the family. Over the meal, the commanding officer relaxes. He kids Ileana about her looks. "Pretty women are more for decoration than for practical use, don't you agree, Archduchess?"

Ileana demurs and points out, "I run the household, but since Anton has left, I've had to learn to repair and maintain the machinery as well."

"Nonsense! An archduchess, a woman, changing a tire, or putting snow tires on? Especially one so pretty? You must think I'm a fool."

"The men who could do that are in the army. If I don't do it, then it doesn't get done."

The other conversations around the table grow quiet. The lighthearted banter takes on a colder edge as the officer scoffs at such an idea. "You couldn't put snow chains on to save your life!"

"But I have," replied Ileana. "I carry the chains in my trunk."

The conversation goes back and forth, tension gathering under the polite words. Finally, the officer throws down a challenge. "Let's go and see which one of us can install a set of chains faster—you or I!"

To everyone's astonishment, Ileana smiles. "Challenge accepted!"

Pandemonium breaks out. The children cheer for their mother, and the staff expresses fear and nervousness—these are Nazi soldiers, after all. But the challenge goes forward, and everyone is involved as the rules are hammered out. Arnold Bitterman, Ileana's secretary and chauffeur, suggests the route—from the front doors, down the drive, around the tree and back—about 50 meters.

Ilse, the governess, says that the chains should be locked in the trunk; Stefan agrees, and insists they use their own jacks. Sandi adds the suggestion about the noise—the chains cannot clank or clatter, they must be properly attached to the tires and must not come off. The children write the rules down as they are agreed on.

The officer, Ileana and the staff, the soldiers and children pile outside with coats, books, scarves, and stopwatches. Stefan blows the starting whistle.

The commander blocks his wheels, dashes to the trunk for the equipment, then hurriedly jacks up the first tire. As he rushes frantically around the car, slipping on the icy snow, Ileana opens her trunk, lays the chains out behind the car and carefully backs onto them. He is just getting the chains out as she latches them onto the tires. By the time she begins driving the course, the officer is still struggling with the second side of his car.

They wait, joking and shivering in the late afternoon light as the commander finishes attaching the chains, then clanks and clunks his way around the course, finishing with a humiliating loss.

He takes the defeat with grace, and afterward, over a hot drink in the drawing room, toasts the archduchess as the "first princess I've ever come to respect as a real man!"

CHAPTER FOURTEEN

Climbing the Staircase

Then he dreamed, and behold, a ladder was set up on the earth,
and its top reached to heaven; and there the angels of God
were ascending and descending on it.
(Genesis 28:12)

leana's sixth and last child, Elisabeth, whom they called "Herzi" (Little Heart), was born on January 15, 1942, at Sonnberg, with the same pot of Romanian soil under the bed as all her brothers and sisters.

By the end of February, Ileana felt recovered enough to travel to Vienna. She and Anton maintained a small apartment there for business they had to conduct. This time she went there for medical checkups for herself and the baby and to run some necessary errands for the household.

While she was there, snowstorms closed the roads outside Vienna, and Ileana was forced to remain in the city. She spent the time catching up with friends and pampering herself a bit. There was talk of the invasion of the Soviet Union, which had filled the newspapers and radio waves since July as Hitler's troops made their slow way forward. Ileana was hungry for news, for Romania's commitment in manpower to this offensive was second only to that of the Wehrmacht* itself, and she was worried about the fate of her countrymen. In spite of the propaganda that was put forward, the rumors said the battle for Moscow had been lost, with more casualties from weather and lack of supplies than from the Soviets defending their capital.

Late one afternoon, Ileana roamed the apartment while Herzi slept, annoyed with herself and restless. It was not just being away from home that upset her, she realized. She'd been to a fashion show that afternoon, and had been shocked and surprised at the grumbling about the restrictions on luxuries like hairdressing salons. "Oddly enough, my indignation was increased rather than lessened when I succumbed and ordered things for myself! I felt ashamed that I, who knew better, should forget even for a moment the sacrifices being made at the front," she wrote.

As she paced the apartment in the fading light, she realized that the root of her dissatisfaction was the desire to be of help.

The phone rang, jarring her out of her reverie. It was an acquaintance who had been visiting a friend at one of the city hospitals. There, she'd discovered a wounded Romanian officer, and wondered if Ileana could visit him. That simple request, which Ileana agreed to immediately, led to her re-emergence into the public sphere, and eventually to her assuming her mother's mantle more completely than either of them would ever have imagined.

There were not one, but two Romanian officers at the makeshift hospital. Ileana discovered that they were part of a thirty-man unit. She managed to track down the other twenty-eight men, as well as others, and visit them.

For the rest of 1942, Ileana divided her time between her family and the wounded. Her work quickly grew to absorb any free moment she had. There was no shortage of Romanian wounded as the Soviet Union's counteroffensive got underway and raged all through the year. Ileana tried to track down every one who came through Vienna. The task grew too large for a single person, so she agitated at the consulate in Vienna and, when they got sick of her, at the legation in Berlin for assistance, funds, and gifts. She made trips to Bucharest to beg for supplies and to consult about methods for more easily tracking the wounded soldiers. As she put it, "I became a beggar of the first rank, regardless of royal dignity!"

But her greatest joy was in talking with the men, writing letters for them, and translating for them and their doctors.

It's easy to think of the princess sitting by a well-made hospital bed with a handsome soldier who is smiling bravely, but, as Ileana wrote, it was seldom so picturesque.

Ileana Remembers

I had to learn to make a supreme effort to realize that the body is only an outward clothing of the soul; that it is not the man himself. I had been asked to look up a soldier who had been a friend of my family for many years, and I had found him. There he lay, who had been strong and cheerful and handsome. He was a skeleton with one leg, and from the stump of the other leg came a nauseating smell of rotting flesh. Because of unhealed wounds and bedsores he could have no clothing on him. Only his eyes in any way resembled the man he had been, and when those eyes recognized me his tears flowed. Filled with compassion and horror I talked with his doctors, who told me it might be possible to save him if a place could be made for him in "the baths."

That was the first time I had heard of the baths, and I immediately used every effort to find out where they were, and then to see that he was moved there as soon as possible. They were not a cheerful sight, those baths! In a cellar whose very air was filled with the stench of decay, soldiers suffering from gangrenous infections in their worst form were placed in cots under moving water. It was a place of living death; and while incredible cures took place, . . . many men died—and not quickly.

I visited our friend there as often as possible, and he proved to be one of those whose wounds finally healed, so that in two months' time he could be moved to another hospital and eventually sent home. . . . Few visitors ever came to the baths, and the soldiers there craved this contact with the outside world almost unbearably.

I had not been sure just what day he would leave, and since I was on another errand in that part of the city I stopped in at the baths to find out if he was still there. He had gone, and his place was already filled by another soldier in even worse condition than his had been, but the man in the next bath spoke to me.

"Ah, Your Highness, we were all hoping that you would not hear your

friend had been moved until you had come once more!" he said. "Without your visits we shall have nothing to look forward to. I had hoped that I might die before they ended!"

The man who had spoken to me was a paraplegic; one who had been wounded in the lung and spine, so that he was almost wholly paralyzed. He had been drafted, wounded, and now lay dying; for the baths failed to help him, and pieces of flesh now and then fell from his legs as they slowly rotted away. For nine more long months he lived; and the last three days of his life I stayed beside him constantly, awaiting his wakening "in a place of light, in a place of greenness, in a place of rest . . ."

For the road of the wounded which I took that snowy day in Vienna brought me many gifts in return for that which I gave of myself. There were many . . . who stood on the threshold of an open door which was still closed to me, and who gave to me something of the vision they were granted of a new heaven and a new earth.

AT CHRISTMAS, Ileana brought some Romanian soldiers to stay at Sonnberg for the holiday. While recovering from a lung infection in early January of 1943, she reflected on how both the men's spirits and their health had improved as a result of the peace and quiet of the area. It wasn't long before she had converted her mother's old suite of rooms into a small hospital, which incidentally solved another nagging problem by ending the unpredictable billets that Sonnberg had endured.

The makeshift hospital in Sonnberg Castle was primarily for convalescent soldiers—most of the men were plastic surgery patients and amputees. They needed time to rest and heal between operations or to adjust to the drastically changed lives ahead of them.

They helped out whenever they could, feeding and caring for each other, making the beds, tidying and cleaning. They helped with table setting and cooking as well, since their army rations had come with them and according to the rationing rules had to be kept separate from the Sonnberg supplies, although a certain amount of sharing did go on.

Ileana and the children spent the summer of 1943 in Romania. They were based both in Bucharest and at Bran, where Ileana had maintained the castle since inheriting it from her mother, five years before.

Conditions in Romania were no better, and perhaps worse, than those in Austria, even though Hitler had moved the Reich to a total war* footing by 1943. Even though there was more news in Romania about the Eastern Front and how the battles were progressing, Ileana was virtually cut off from news from Western Europe and her friends and family in England, France, and Spain. Because both Romania and the Reich controlled all communication, very little about the turning tide of the war leaked through to them. Ileana heard triumphant Nazi accounts of the Allied failure in the Dieppe Raid in 1942, but news of the surrender of the German and Italian troops in North Africa in May of 1943 was ruthlessly suppressed, as was that of the Allied advance through Italy and Italy's surrender that same summer.

In spite of her lack of news, it was a busy summer, because Ileana was still preoccupied with the problems of the wounded Romanian soldiers. She spent much of her time meeting with government and Red Cross officials to extend the work she was doing, and before she left she had the authorization to travel anywhere in the Reich, Poland, or Czechoslovakia to find them.

Now that her nephew Mihai was on the throne, Ileana was expected and eager to do her duty as a princess of the country. Early on the morning of August 1, she and her secretary, Arnold Bitterman, set off to visit a friend before opening a school in Ploesti, near the richest of Romania's oil fields. Having witnessed the effects of the massive American bombing raid on the oil refinery plants outside town, Ileana returned to Bran shaken and thoughtful.

She visited her mother's most cherished friend and the man she trusted above any other—the "Good Man" of her childhood, Prince Barbu Stirbey, who had returned to Romania when Carol abdicated. She explained to him that while the work she was doing in Austria was necessary and satisfying, Romania suffered too, and her heart was, as always, with her country. In addition, she confided, the increasing indoctrination of the Reich was beginning to wear on her. The children were exposed to it in school, it was in all the papers and promoted everywhere. She didn't want her children growing up as good little Nazis. Ileana objected to the totalitarianism of the Nazis and to the methods they used to ensure obedience and loyalty.

There was also the expense of running two full estates. She couldn't spend all her time at either, but the staff and bills had to be paid at both. She didn't know what to do—her heart said one thing, her mind said another, and her duty was both to the soldiers in Austria and to Romania itself.

"But you must decide what you feel yourself to be. Are you Austrian, German, or Romanian?" he asked her finally.

"I am a Romanian," she replied.

"Then stand by your choice!" he exclaimed. "*Be* a Romanian!"

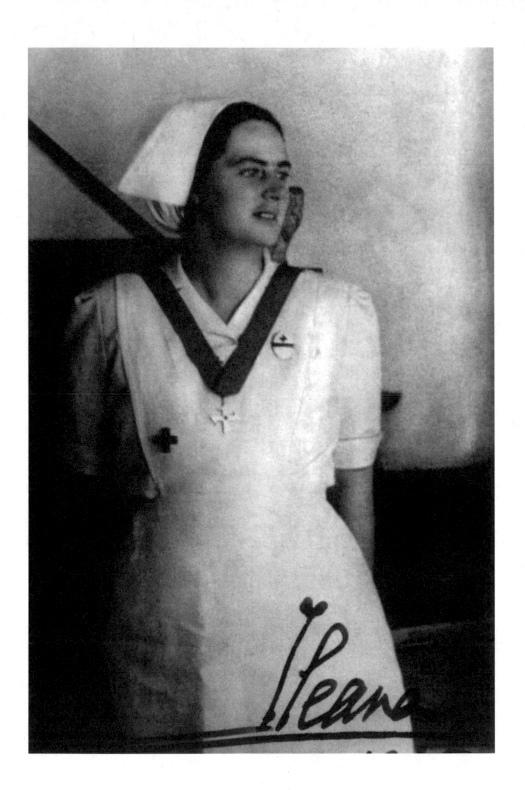

Ileana

Section IV

Romania in Turmoil

Archduchess Ileana's Red Cross card

TIMELINE 1944–1947

YEAR	COUNTRY	EVENT
1944	Austria/ Romania	Ileana trapped in Romania when Hungarian border closes, works at Brasov Red Cross station; establishes Hospital of the Queen's Heart in Bran; Anton Habsburg released from German Air Force
	Romania	King Mihai arrests Ion Antonescu, declares ceasefire, signs armistice with Allies; Soviets invade
	Europe	Rome falls (mainland Italy now defended by Nazi troops); Nazi forces occupy Hungary; Battle of Normandy ("D-Day"), Allied invasion of Europe begins; defeat of German forces at Bagran by Soviets; Greece liberated, begins Civil War; Battle of the Bulge (Ardennes Offensive) begins
	Pacific	Capture of Marshall Islands; US invades Saipan; Battle of Guam
1945	Romania	Communist government imposed by USSR; Anton Habsburg placed under house arrest; Ileana becomes member of underground
	Europe	Battle of the Bulge continues; Soviet Army liberates Auschwitz; Yalta Conference; Dresden firebombed; Mussolini executed; Hitler commits suicide; end of war in Europe
	Pacific	Battle of Iwo Jima; liberation of Manila; Battle of Okinawa; atomic bombs dropped on Hiroshima and Nagasaki, surrender of Japan, end of WWII
	USA	FDR dies, Truman president
1946	Romania	Expansion of Hospital of the Queen's Heart; Anton released from house arrest; Ion Antonescu tried and executed; continued Soviet occupation
	USA/USSR	Cold War begins
	World	United Nations formed; League of Nations disbanded
1947	Romania	Arrests and executions of top-ranking Romanians; Ileana and family exiled; Mihai forced to abdicate and exiled; formation of Romanian People's Republic
	Britain	Princess Elizabeth marries Prince Phillip, Duke of Edinburgh

CHAPTER FIFTEEN

Being a Romanian

Give us this day our daily bread. (Matthew 6:11)

In September of 1943, Ileana kissed Stefan, Minola, and Sandi goodbye and left them with friends in Brasov to attend Romanian schools, while she returned to Sonnberg with Niki, Magi, and Herzi. She hired a doctor and a nurse for the hospital at Sonnberg, and spent most of the fall and winter of 1943 traveling around the Reich.

Living in a country at war is never safe, and Ileana had her share of scares and narrow escapes even before she began her work for the soldiers; but with her increased travel, she encountered far more risk than she'd ever experienced before. Additionally, with the tide of the war changing in the Allies' favor, the bombing raids into Nazi territory increased in frequency and intensity.

She learned to travel with hand luggage only and was always prepared if a station had been bombed out of existence. She never wandered far from the train on its stops. If the air raid siren sounded, the train would leave the station as quickly as possible in order to avoid being blown to bits; if you weren't on it, so much the worse for you!

She grew accustomed to the train stopping in the middle of nowhere, day or night, and having to jump out, whatever the time of year or weather, to lie in the fields by the tracks, cowering under what little cover was available, while planes streaked overhead and bombs exploded nearby.

By 1944, five years of war were grating on everyone. Shortages were worse, rationing was tightened, bombings increased, and repairs were slow to nonexistent, since all available resources, both materials and man-power, were dedicated to the war effort. People were required to take in refugees whose homes had been destroyed, and Sonnberg was no excep-tion. Tempers were short, and squabbles, both serious and trivial, were frequent.

In addition, the hospital, while successful, had its own problems. Addiction to morphine was common, and many of the men were depressed over their injuries, anxious about their future, and in constant pain, all of which added to the stress of the situation. Despite all the treatment and aid the staff could give, some men died, which affected everyone.

The longer Ileana remained in Austria, the more certain she became that the family needed to return to Romania.

In early March, 1944, Ileana took the younger children to Romania by her usual route—train from Vienna to Hungary and through Hungary into Romania. Her intention was to leave the three younger ones with their older siblings, while she returned to Austria to wrap up loose ends. Then she would pack up Sonnberg and return for good. However, just after she arrived in Romania, Hitler invaded Hungary and the border snapped shut, trapping her in her homeland with many things unfinished.

Expecting a stay of only a few weeks, Ileana and her family moved into the gatehouse at the foot of Bran Castle. The castle itself, never meant as a full-time residence, was unheated and impossible to live in during the winters.

Once the children were settled, she looked to her people, to give help where they needed it most. Hordes of refugees poured into and through the country from Bessarabia and the easternmost portions of Romania, mostly by train. The railway pressed anything available into service. Passenger cars, freight cars, and cattle boxes overcrowded with desperate, hungry, shocked people moved through Brasov at all hours. A Red Cross canteen in the station distributed tea, soup, and bread to the crowds.

One cold, sunny morning in late March, Ileana pushed through the soldiers, women and children, officials and stray dogs crowding the old, worn platforms and waiting rooms. She shouldered her way into the canteen, where she met a tall fair-haired woman who looked as if she had no time for pampered princesses who couldn't scrub a dirty pot or lift a heavy kettle.

Ileana, still painfully shy, quailed under this direct and dismissive glare. "I felt small and incompetent," she wrote, "while outside I felt as though my hands and feet were suddenly abnormally large and completely awkward," but she managed to stammer out a desire to help.

Mrs. Podgoreanu directed her to the canteen window, to dispense tea to the troop train just pulling into the station.

The next trains proved Ileana's mettle. The cars were packed with dirty, tired, and hungry people who had grabbed whatever belongings they could as they fled. Ileana scrambled through the crowded cars, arms laden with baskets of bread, noting the people who were ill or injured. She struggled past a cow standing next to a handsome bronze lamp, and laughed at a hen nesting in a Louis XV chair. On the line furthest from the station platform, on a train from Jassy, she climbed into a cattle car, where she found "a woman in labor, an old woman attending her, and the two of them surrounded by the rest of the family as well as by a cow, a few pigs and some annoyed and cackling hens." The baby girl was born and baptized in the station, with Ileana as godmother.

That same day, Ileana was stopped on the platform by an old friend, General Nicolae Tatranu. He was looking for a place to house a dispensary for the refugees. Would Domnitza be willing to organize it, in cooperation with the head of the military hospital downtown? Ileana agreed, and they found an ideal spot—a closed restaurant next to the station.

While the dispensary was being organized and staffed, she continued to hand out the milk, soup, and tea, jostling with starving crowds who in their need forgot all human charity.

Ileana ran across old friends and acquaintances at the station—many whom she'd known in Jassy when she was a refugee. One of them, her childhood friend Iona Perticari, arrived near Pascha. Ileana, overjoyed her friend had survived, found Iona and her family a place in Bran, along with other refugees.

But not all of the heartache ended so well.

୧୨୧୧ ୧୨୧୧ ୧୨୧ Imagine This ୧୨୧୧ ୧୨୧୧ ୧୨୧

I leana steps out from the canteen. The evening is quiet, the sky clear, its color that dark bluey-black that occurs just before dark. It's pleasant, and she breathes deeply, enjoying the crisp air. A man dodging through the crowds attracts her attention.

"Stop him! He's a thief, he's stolen my bag," yells a second man as he bursts through a group of people, scattering them. He catches up to the first, and snatches at the suitcase, eyes wide, face tight with desperation. People stop them and gather around.

Ileana listens as they argue. The first man, his suit ragged but shoes shining, sounds a bit too bluff and scornful to Ileana's ear. The second man, in a worn suit, with a frayed collar and old, stained tie, is by contrast almost hysterical. His voice sounds higher than an opera soprano's, and his words tumble over themselves, he speaks so quickly.

She edges closer as a gendarme shoulders his way through the crowd. He listens to the claims and counterclaims. Something obviously doesn't sound right to him either, for he instructs both men to come to the police station.

Ileana trails along, her suspicions aroused, wanting to help if she can.

"It's simple," says the gendarme, finally. "Tell us what's in the suitcase, we'll open it and see who's right."

The second man pales even further. "No!" he barks. "I—I c-can't tell you."

"He's lying, you see," says the first man.

It isn't right, Ileana thinks. The first man is too bluff, too full of bravado, and the second—what could be in the case that he wouldn't want anyone to know?

The officer gestures to Ileana, and they leave the room.

"It's odd, Domnitza," he says.

She nods. "Yes. I think the suitcase belongs to the man with the frayed collar, but why would he be so frightened?"

The gendarme waves a hand and laughs. "The case is full of contraband. The problem is how to get him to prove the case is his, so that we can give it back to him and charge the other fellow."

"Let me try," says Ileana. She re-enters the room and draws the shabby man aside. "We do want to help. We think the case is yours," she says gently, "but unless you tell us what's in it, we'll have to assume that the case really is his."

The man in the shabby suit turns his head away, but not before Ileana sees the shine of tears. He caresses the case with one finger, shakes his head.

After more persuasion, the man finally gives her the key to the case.

The gendarme opens the bag, and she, the officer and the thief gasp and draw back in horror. The owner turns away, strangling a sob.

Curled up as if asleep, clad in a ragged gray suit, lies the body of a little boy, no more than two, Ileana thinks.

It is the man's son. He died on the train. Rather than abandon him or bury him where they would never return, the man and his wife decided to take the body with them so they might visit his grave.

Ileana and the police officer trade glances.

"Will you, Domnitza?" he asks. Ileana nods. She makes arrangements for the burial, takes the man's name and destination address, and promises to send photos of the gravesite when the boy is buried. Then she sees the man back onto the train just as it pulls out of the station.

ILEANA SPLIT HER TIME between the train station and the military hospital, where she worked as a nurse. Finally, in May, the border reopened and she was able to make a rushed trip to Sonnberg. There she tied up the loose ends of her work and was able to spend some time with Anton, who was home on a quick leave.

CHAPTER SIXTEEN

Spitalul Inima Reginei
(The Hospital of the Queen's Heart)

My heart is ready, O God, my heart is ready;
I will sing and give praise in my glory.
(Psalm 108:1)

n her return to Bran, Ileana was asked to help establish a hospital annex. Brasov was an important industrial center, so air raids on the city were frequent and intense. Air-raid shelters were nothing more than makeshift trenches dug into hillsides, and it was common for the staff and patients to flee for the shelters while bombs fell around them, as happened one Pascha day.

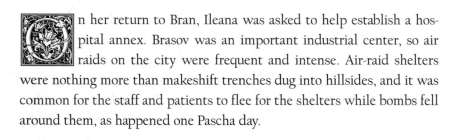

Ileana Remembers

The service over, I went to take a share of the eggs and gifts to the men who could not leave their beds. It was at this moment that the General's aide-de-camp came and told me enemy planes were heading for Brasov. . . .

I stepped out into the courtyard to make my way to the dugouts on the hillside just as the first wave of planes was overhead. They were silver and beautiful against the blue sky, so that for an instant they seemed no part of war and destruction. Then suddenly the air was rent by a tremendous sound, and engulfing dust and acrid fumes seemed to surround us from all sides. It was as if a huge, impersonal hand pushed me down flat on my face. Stunned and deafened for a moment, I was roused by the terrified shrieks of a woman whom I saw running downhill and away from safety, carrying a child in her arms. I scrambled to my feet and caught up with her. There was no time to argue even if she could have heard me, so I chose an easier way to stop her. I snatched the child from her arms and turned and ran up the hill, while she followed me, still screaming. We reached the dugouts and jumped into a trench just as the second wave of bombs fell. When the dust cleared a little for the second time I found myself surrounded by weeping women and terrified young girls. I was a little surprised to find that I felt no fear and that I could repeat the 91st Psalm. Slowly it calmed the others, and they quieted. It was then that my own self-control was most threatened, for I saw when I opened my eyes that on each side of me they had taken hold of my long head [nursing] veil, and had spread it over their heads as if for protection, as if they were indeed my children.

How much time passed before the raid ended is no longer clear to me: there were to be so many raids!

THE MOST SERIOUSLY WOUNDED couldn't be moved and so risked death during every air raid, as did those who stayed with them. They needed a quiet place further from the center of the raids, where the danger was less, and their condition could stabilize before surgery.

Bran, located fifty miles from Brasov, had a hospital that might serve the purpose. Ileana approached the mayor, who was also the doctor and owned the hospital, but he turned her down flat.

Furious, burning with indignation, she stood outside and remembered vividly "the pandemonium during the bombings, in the Brasov hospital. . . . Impotent rage filled my breast. . . . Then my troubled eyes fell upon a green and pleasant spot across the river. It was narrow, fronted by a row of ancient willow trees, their gnarled, exposed roots clutching the riverbank, and backed by the gentle, wooded foothills of the Carpathians. What an ideal spot for a hospital, I thought, if only there was a building on it!"

There wasn't, and the land was under cultivation, so she had to look elsewhere. Fortunately, the village priest donated an empty schoolhouse, and Ileana put Iona in charge of organizing and fitting out the annex.

It opened and was operating in a remarkably short time, but there were problems. The building had no running water. Every drop—and hospitals use a lot of water—had to be carried in. There were no operating facilities, so while the men who had been treated could recover, it still meant that pre-operative patients had to remain in Brasov, in the "Ward of Terror."

From the moment she stood outside the door of the doctor-mayor's hospital, Ileana knew she wanted to build a proper hospital. But building one from scratch is no easy feat. In addition to the wartime shortages of building materials, labor, and supplies, Ileana was not, despite her royal status, a public institution. She would have to rely on her own resources to build it.

She had the property; the land with the willows belonged to her. But it was farmland she'd rented out, and there were crops growing on it. After the harvest, perhaps.

The army had portable barracks—perhaps she could buy one or two. But how would she get beds and linens? Who would do the plumbing? Who would put in the electricity? Where could she obtain furnishings, bed linens, and bandages? The list got longer the more she thought.

Ileana, while a princess, wasn't all that rich. While she did have income from several sources, most of those sources were land, and as war-damaged as any other property in Romania. The land didn't provide the same income as in prewar times. And Ileana didn't pay only for the upkeep of Bran and Sonnberg and her family. She, like her mother, had "adopted" a number of needy people, placing them on her staff. Also, she always had a generous heart and would help any who asked, whether they asked for a bandage, a willing ear, or a gift of money.

What she couldn't pay for, she reasoned, she would trust to God to provide, out of His boundless generosity and mercy. She didn't know how generous or merciful He could be, but she was about to learn. She dug out a valuable bracelet, determined to sell it so she could start the project.

Trusting in God was the right thing to do. She told General Tatranu about her idea and how she would pay for it. He demanded she put away the bracelet, claiming gruffly that he could get not one, but two used army barracks for her. The tenants to whom she'd rented the land insisted that they be allowed to absorb the loss of their crop as an offering to her hospital.

Overjoyed, Ileana went to see a Colonel Serbu in a nearby town. He was in charge of an ammunitions factory that had a small cabinetry workshop on the side. She asked if he could supply, at cost, the furnishings for the hospital. He agreed, and further, offered her two almost new army barracks in exchange for General Tatranu's old ones. In addition, he appointed himself construction supervisor and worked closely with the laborers on the building.

Finally, the colonel offhandedly donated an entire operating room to the project. He had planned to use it for the dispensary at the factory, but it had never been installed. All he asked was that the hospital treat his employees at no charge. Ileana agreed gratefully.

With the colonel supervising the construction, Ileana was able to concentrate on obtaining supplies, which seemed to appear just when she needed them most—even if they weren't quite what she'd envisioned. The nurses' uniforms, instead of being plain grey with white aprons and bibs, were sewn from donated fabric in a variety of colors, which, in addition to designating the nurses' status—brick red for graduate nurses, royal blue for students, and yellow for ward maids—enlivened the hospital and raised the patients' spirits.

In July, Ileana and the children received a wonderful surprise. Anton came to Bran for good after being released from the German Luftwaffe.

He arrived in time for the hospital blessing on July 22. The hospital was still incomplete but already had an icon in every room. Ileana chose the date specifically because it was her mother's nameday, and she called the hospital *Spitalul Inima Reginei*—the Hospital of the Queen's Heart.

In her will, Queen Marie had requested that her heart be removed from her body and laid to rest at Balcic. When, in 1940, Romania had lost that section of country to Bulgaria, Ileana had moved the heart and installed it in a niche in the mountain behind Bran's village church. She yearned to erect a suitable memorial besides the small chapel that protected the niche. Soon after her vision on the riverbank, she realized that the best way

The Hospital of the Queen's Heart

to memorialize Marie was a "place where those in pain could find comfort and healing."

The day was a wonder for Ileana, and the hospital was ready for the first patients' arrival on September 8, 1944. With them they brought rumors and wild surmises about recent events in Bucharest and what they would mean for the country.

In August 1944, twenty-two-year-old Mihai, the figurehead king, had arrested Ion Antonescu and sought an armistice with the Allies. This should have ended the war for the Romanians, although the Western Allies would continue to fight until May of 1945. But the Soviets—Romania's supposed allies—instead of moving in to help repel the German forces, invaded, reporting that they'd "captured" villages and announcing the taking of between 140,000 and 600,000 prisoners—very few of whom were ever released.

All through the country during late August and early September, confusion reigned—no one seemed sure who was an ally and who was an enemy. Fighting broke out in and around Bran and Brasov, and orders were issued to arrest all Germans.

❧❧❧ Imagine This ❧❧❧

S itta, as the family calls Queen Mother Helen, descends the stairs, one hand resting lightly on the dark, polished wooden banister. Ileana smiles delightedly and moves forward, her hands outstretched. "Sitta! It's such a pleasure to see you. I hope you're well, I've been worried."

The Queen Mother nods as she grasps Ileana's hands and they embrace, but there's stiffness in her body and a distance to her that Ileana has never felt before. They're not the best of friends—they're too different to be close—but Ileana and Sitta had always felt comfortable together.

"Is Mihai here also? Is he well?"

"He's here, but he's busy right now," says Sitta. "He asked me to come and speak with you. Will you take tea? Or coffee?"

Ileana nods and Sitta calls for coffee. They sit down and talk briefly of inconsequentials. Ileana asks about Sitta's family—with the upheavals in Greece and the occupation by Italy, they had been scattered all over.

Once the coffee is served, Sitta leans forward. "And you? How are you and your family?"

"That's why I came. You must know about the danger we're in, Sitta." Helen nods—of course she knows. The Soviets have declared all royalty enemies of the people. The papers have been full of it, and the talk has been of little else.

"It's not just that, though. The Soviets have issued orders to arrest all Germans, and that means the children and Anton. Even I am at risk, since I came into Romania on a German passport.

"Can Mihai not do something for us? There are rumors that Anton is to be arrested and shipped to Russia, or that he will be shot. I've heard that the children and I will be confined to a monastery or sent to Russia as well. You know what that means!" Ileana leans forward and grasps her ex-sister-in-law's wrist.

"It's not just for me I ask. My hospital can't yet do without me, and the children—oh, the children, Sitta! How can I protect them?" Her voice unsteady, she stops and clasps her hands tightly in her lap.

Helen shifts in her chair and clears her throat. "Ileana, the king is— oh, how I hate to say this—the king is in great danger. You're right.

The Soviets hate us, and they would take any opportunity to topple Mihai from his throne." She pauses and looks away, as if she can't meet Ileana's eyes.

"Mihai can do nothing right now. He's hanging on by a thread, and—" Sitta puts her coffee down and toys with the cake on her plate. "I think it would be better if we were not to see you or have any contact with you at all. It's just too dangerous."

Ileana sits in shock—the hurt goes all the way into her. She feels as if she's received a heavy blow to her stomach.

"I'm sorry," Sitta continues. "I truly am, please forgive me. This is a time when we should support each other, but right now anything, anything at all could give the Soviets an excuse to remove Mihai, and then we'd all be facing disaster or worse.

"Knowing that Anton is German now that Austria is part of Germany, and that the children are as well, could be the one thing that would give the Soviets the courage to take his throne."

Numb, feeling disconnected from the reality of the drawing room around her, the sun pouring in the windows, the quiet music from the radio in the background, Ileana puts her cup down and rises to her feet. How she keeps her balance is a mystery to her, for her head is whirling and her soul aches.

"Of course. I understand completely, Sitta. I hadn't thought it through, but you're right."

And the worst of it is, Ileana does understand. It doesn't help the hurt, the shock, but she is a realist and knows that Sitta is only speaking the truth. Anything that could taint Mihai has to be avoided, and since Romania is now an Ally, fighting the Germans, even her very presence in the house endangers him and their country.

"I'll leave now, and—" She trails off for a moment. "I have another appointment, and I mustn't be late. Please excuse me for such a short visit." Ileana gathers up her purse while Sitta summons the maid to see her relative out. Blinded by tears, Ileana barely notices the hot summer sun as she flees into her car.

FROM THE PALACE ILEANA WENT TO A FRIEND'S HOUSE, where she was introduced to a high-ranking Romanian officer, General Aldea. While Ileana never revealed publicly the true reason for the meeting, from her later statements it seems fair to assume that in addition to other business they discussed, the general recruited her into the underground, to fight the Soviet communist takeover of Romania. It wouldn't have been a hard sell for someone like Ileana. Aldea was also able to get Anton's arrest orders amended to house arrest.

The very real danger Ileana was in was brought home to her when the general insisted on providing an armed guard for her return to Bran. Stopped several times on the drive home, they were challenged and threatened. It was clear to Ileana that without their bodyguard, they'd have been roughed up, even arrested or shot.

CHAPTER SEVENTEEN

War's End, Sorrow's Beginning

Keep me, O Lord, from the hand of the sinner;
Deliver me from unjust men
Who plotted to trip up my steps.
(Psalm 139:5)

oviet troops continued moving into Romania through the fall. They passed through Bran sometimes singly, often twenty or thirty together, sometimes as many as a hundred. They came on foot, in carts or trucks, stealing what they wanted. Hoping to mitigate the worst of the plundering and terror, the villagers set aside some of their food and cattle and hid the rest. Ileana parked the family and hospital cars in the garden, where they were covered with branches and leaves.

The women and girls hid as best they could. The situation was so terrifying that Ileana dared not step out of the castle or the hospital while troops were passing through, and her daughters were confined to the inner courtyard until the soldiers had gone.

In spite of the precautions, there was no escaping the soldiers. They had no qualms about tearing houses and people apart to find and take what they wanted. Women of all ages—even old babas—were subjected to unspeakable cruelty. Ileana recalled one elderly woman, brought to the hospital by neighbors when they found her stuffed into a bread oven. She had been so abused by the Soviet soldiers that she died, broken in body and mind.

For the princess, "the terrifying part was the methodical brutality with which everything was done. The Russians did not seem to enjoy either their power or their sins." She wrote that they seemed to be "robbed of their very souls," and while the soldiers never came up to the castle or crossed the bridge from the main road to the hospital, the fear that they would was always present.

In spite of the invasion by the Soviet "allies," the little hospital in Bran flourished. More and more serious cases were sent from Brasov, and the people of the area began coming to Spitalul Inima Reginei for treatment. By the middle of the fall, they had about fifty civilian men admitted and had treated many more on an outpatient basis. When it was safe, Ileana roamed the steep, wooded hills around Bran to help the women who couldn't be admitted to her hospital, for there was no women's ward, and many couldn't afford the civilian hospital across the river.

There was enough need that finally, a doctor and a medical student were stationed at the hospital. It wasn't long before they, too, were tramping the hills with Ileana. But this was only a stopgap solution.

The point was driven home one afternoon just after the New Year when they had to drive a dangerously ill woman in childbirth to Brasov. This

Archduchess Ileana with Gypsy women

was normally a couple of hours' drive on rough roads, but the heavy snow-fall and drifts that had isolated Bran made the trip a nightmare. It was late at night when they finally arrived at the hospital, where the mother was treated and delivered a healthy child.

Isolated as they were in the valley, with the passes so clogged with snow, it's not surprising that most of the political events seemed to pass Ileana and Bran by. But when the Soviets imposed a communist government on Romania in March of 1945, the repercussions and terror reached everyone, no matter how remote or isolated they were by the terrain and weather.

"People's tribunals" were set up to investigate allegations of war crimes. Anyone could be arrested for speaking out against the Party or its policies, and over the next few years, all property and goods were appropriated by the government.

The hospital benefited from this, for many of the supply houses gave Ileana equipment, irreplaceable with wartime shortages, rather than hand it over to the Soviets. Even some of the government ministries authorized special shipments of supplies and drugs to Spitalul Inima Reginei rather than have them fall into Soviet hands.

Courtesy of Jim Krichbaum

The interior of Bran Castle

For Ileana, this was a precarious and heartbreaking time. As a member of the royal family, with connections and friendships in the ruling class going back to her childhood in Jassy, she was powerless as old and dear friends were arrested and disappeared—to torture, into Soviet Russia, or to their graves. It meant watching as minor Communist Party officials arrested and confiscated the property of the villagers she'd known for years, many of whom were deprived of jobs and homes for having held the wrong job during the war or for speaking too freely.

In addition, as a princess, Ileana was automatically assumed to be an enemy of the newly communist state. She and the family could be arrested at any time, taken to the Soviet Union, and never be heard from again.

People showed up at the castle at odd times of the night—to be hidden and moved out of the country before the authorities found them. In the eccentrically built castle, Ileana and Anton had lots of nooks and crannies in which to secrete political fugitives.

Yet Ileana's work in the hospital and around Bran and Brasov was famous enough that high-ranking ministers of the government came to see and left impressed. One, Emile Bodnaras, the Secretary of the Communist Party and later Secretary General of the Presidency, toured the hospital just before the communist takeover. He didn't mince words, telling Ileana, "My opinion of you and of your work has changed. . . . When we come to power, remember me. I will do all that I can to help you."

While officially she was regarded with suspicion, and twenty-three-year-old King Mihai still maintained his distance, informally Ileana's dedication, warmth, and concern won her friends on all sides—communist and rebel alike. She was in a position where, at considerable risk to herself, she could do a lot of good, and she did it—whether it was begging the minister of health for supplies for the hospital, hiding "enemies of the state," or appealing to the head of the government for those who'd been arrested.

Imagine This

Blackout regulations are still in effect, even though the war is over, and the street is dark. The sky is overcast, so not even the stars and moon lend light to this dangerous trip. Curfew is in effect, and if the wrong person comes along, Ileana could be arrested. She walks rapidly from the church, where she's said a quick prayer and lit a candle, to a certain street corner. It may be just her imagination, but the shadows feel thicker here, somehow, even though there are no street lights to cast them.

A car pulls up. *Jesus Christ, Son of God, have mercy on me.* A deep breath, as she checks the license number. It's the one she was told to watch for. She steps from the curb as the back door opens. In spite of her fear and the sinister appearance of the men in the front seat, she can't help a rueful smile as she settles into the empty backseat and closes the door. This is the kind of thing she and Papa used to talk about when they read the Bulldog Drummond* stories, years ago. How extraordinary that she would actually be living in such a world!

The car pulls away, its motor a quiet rumble, more felt than heard. A turn to the right. They drive straight along the road for a while, then make a left. Another left and right in quick succession, but she's too nervous to keep them straight. *Jesus Christ, Son of God, have mercy on me.* She doesn't dare write the directions down; the big man sitting shotgun—and doesn't that have a whole new meaning for her now!— glances in the rearview mirror every so often. Tearing the notebook out of her hands would be the least he'd do. Another right. The men look so threatening—wide shoulders, thick necks. All she can see is their silhouettes, no real details. They're big and bearlike. Are they Russian? She hasn't the nerve to speak and find out. *Jesus Christ, Son of God, have mercy on me.*

The car purrs quietly, tires whispering along the pavement. There's no other sound on this dark, sinister night. An occasional bump jars her as they hit a pothole or a crack in the road. A left, another left, a right. She doesn't know why she's still paying attention, she lost track long ago. She glances out the window, but it's too dark to see landmarks.

Is she really going to meet the man she's scheduled to see? Or will these men take her to prison? Will they drive into the country and put a gun to her head? She'd never be found. Poor Anton, poor children, they'll be arrested without her. Mihai can't do anything, he's as powerless as she is. Will she disappear into the Soviet Union?

She twists her hands together nervously. The Jesus Prayer, normally so calming, does nothing to stem her anxiety.

The men in the front seat are silent. She thinks of more detective stories—they're her favorite kind of book, and she's read a lot of them. She glances out the window again. She can see the bulk of buildings, so they must still be in the city.

Eventually the car pulls up. She is handed out, gently, and is left in front of a pleasant villa surrounded by a garden. To either side are more houses and gardens. The front door opens, spilling warm yellow light onto the walk and the plants of the garden. Standing in the doorway, hands out in welcome, a smile on their faces, are Ileana's contacts—Emile Bodnaras, one of the most powerful members of the ruling Romanian Communist Party, and his wife, waiting to welcome her as if this were nothing more than a pleasant evening visit.

It wasn't just a visit, though. Ileana had come to beg for the lives of men she had known all her life, men who had fought for Romania through two world wars, and who had, in her opinion, done nothing worse than live for their country. She later denied having much influence in the final decision, but it is a matter of record that the sentences for these men were commuted to life imprisonment. She wasn't as fortunate in many other cases.

CHAPTER EIGHTEEN

Tightropes & Undergrounds

I lifted my eyes to the mountains;
From where shall my help come?
My help comes from the Lord,
Who made heaven and earth.
(Psalm 120:1)

ut having "friends" in high places didn't make Ileana's life any easier. If anything, it worsened it, as people questioned her loyalties and she became known, along with her sister Lisabeta, as one of "the Red Aunts." People whispered that she cooperated with the communists, that she was a close friend of the ruling cadre.

While Ileana used her sympathetic communist acquaintances to obtain supplies and equipment for the hospital and to beg for people's lives and freedom, in truth she was no sympathizer. Ileana despised what the communist regime was doing to her country. She fought against it from the start with every resource at her command.

She hired a married couple, friends of hers, to run her farm outside Brasov after the government fired the man and confiscated their home because he had been a minor bureaucrat during the war. The food produced by the farm fed the hospital, and there was usually enough extra to feed the "criminals" that Ileana and Anton were constantly hiding in the hospital, at the castle, and in the woods nearby.

The communists were more than happy, on one hand, to exploit what they could of her reluctant dealings with them, and on the other, to slap her down to remind her who was boss. But they got overconfident, and in the summer and fall of 1945, their actions brought about first a spiritual epiphany for Ileana, and second, her reconciliation with Mihai.

Her estrangement from Mihai and Sitta was a source of unending grief for Ileana. She understood the reasons for it, for Mihai's position as king was even more precarious than her own, and he needed all the security he could find in order to work for his people. But it hurt, and when the government refused to allow her presence at the seven-year memorial service for her mother in July of 1945, her heart broke.

Ileana Remembers

I remember especially one day . . . in July, 1945, when a great sorrow had come to me in the form of what seemed to me a terrible injustice. I had been excluded from being present in Curtea de Arges, where the seven years' memorial service was being held for my mother. . . . I felt, this I cannot endure. This is too much. I cannot bear it.

So I sought refuge again at the little chapel, seeking for strength to bear the unbearable; for even physically I felt that I could not endure the pain. Then my eyes fell upon the eternal unmoved perfection of the mountain. So long had it stood there just like that—so very long: even before history began. It had been unchanged and unhurt by human strife and endeavor, by humiliations, hopes, and despairs. How small I and my pain were! And suddenly I understood that such things did not matter; that they were of no importance at all. Such things were there simply to be overcome; they were put in our way for us to use in building the staircase of life. On each one we could mount one step higher until finally we attained the Mountain, the eternal reality of living.

I mention this moment because it was such a deep and real experience that it was one of the greatest events of my life: a day of revelation when I definitely opened another door and stepped forward. It was then also that I better knew and understood my mother, and how she had been able to build from anguish and sorrow a stairway to attainment.

FOR THE REST OF HER LIFE, Ileana understood that nothing that happens in this life is wasted—all can be used to grow closer to God, to submit to His will and to praise and glorify His name. It was knowledge she could use now to bolster herself against the pain of Mihai's estrangement and the communists' lies about her. It was knowledge she would need desperately in just a few years.

In the fall, the issue of the children's education came up again. Because of the communist antipathy toward Germany, all rights to education had been revoked for German citizens, including Ileana's family. For the younger children, this wasn't a problem, since the Bran schoolmaster decreed that since he hadn't received anything official, there was no ban. However, Stefan was high school age and couldn't attend the Bran school or the high school in Brasov.

A former aide sat on the Board of Trustees of a nearby military academy, and Ileana asked him if Stefan could attend there. She let the former aide handle the arrangements, preferring to stay in the background. On the first day of school, the minister of war was there to welcome Stefan and to announce that the king himself had consented to the arrangement. Ileana, delighted, wrote Mihai to thank him. He let her know in no uncertain terms that he had not known about it and had not been consulted.

What Ileana didn't know was that the king was on strike. For months he had refused to sign the bills passed in parliament. While this didn't stop the communists from enacting legislation, the government saw Stefan's education as an ideal opportunity to exploit Mihai's relationship with Stefan and the school for propaganda purposes. When the king found out, he was livid and demanded Stefan's withdrawal.

All through September and October, Ileana attempted to meet with Mihai to explain the situation, but was unsuccessful. Finally, through intermediaries, King Mihai ordered Stefan out of the school. While she might have disobeyed her nephew, she couldn't disobey her king, so she made arrangements to bring Stefan home. That night before he left, she prayed for an answer. Finally she said, "Thy will be done—if Stefan is to attend, then he will stay. If it's not right, he will have to go." She fell into a deep, restful sleep to wake, the following morning, to an unusually early, tremendous snowfall. Not even sleds could be used to travel.

Ileana used the respite, which she regarded as a minor miracle, to pester for an audience with Mihai. Finally he agreed, and near Christmas, the roads cleared enough to allow her to travel to Sinaia. Once in his presence, Ileana and Mihai discovered that the estrangement had been fomented and encouraged by the government to keep them separate. Ileana had been constantly and completely misrepresented to her nephew by the communists. She was delighted at the reconciliation, and not only because Stefan could stay in school. "We were together again in fact, as we had always been in mind and affection."

The communists had overstepped themselves this time. Instead of using Ileana and Stefan to manipulate the king's image and drive the aunt and nephew further apart, their propaganda efforts had backfired and brought the two closer together. But it was symptomatic of Ileana's life: nothing was as it seemed. On the surface, things were normal as she raised her children, worked in the hospital, and communicated with Mihai and Sitta. But at the same time, under cover of darkness, in nooks and crannies of the castle, her life was filled with the intrigue and tension of a spy or war novel. But for Ileana, the stakes weren't just a good read—one wrong step and she and her family would plunge to their deaths.

CHAPTER NINETEEN

Life under the Communists

Keep me as the apple of Your eye;
In the shelter of Your wings, You will shelter me
From the face of the ungodly who trouble me.
(Psalm 16:8–9)

t wasn't only Ileana the communists were after—it was every-one, and Ileana helped whomever she could. This sometimes landed her and her supplicant in bizarre situations.

Imagine This

It's a quiet afternoon. No emergencies, nothing out of the ordinary, and the patients are all well cared for by the nursing staff. Ileana has decided to divide the recent shipment of flour into the staff rations, and the dispensary is the only room large enough to hold all the flour, scales, and bags. Ileana and her helpers joke and laugh as the flour is weighed and bagged.

"Domnitza! Domnitza!" Work stops at the frantic note in the voice from the hall.

"That's Dan Tomascu," says Ileana, alarmed at the panic in his voice. "What could be wrong?" A chill slides down her back. It's a rhetorical question. Dan, a villager and a former tutor of Stefan's, is well known and liked in the village, and most people are aware that he's no friend to the communists. It's likely, she thinks, that the police have finally uncovered one or another of his activities.

He bursts into the room, chest heaving and eyes popping. Ileana drops her flour scoop and strides over to him.

Between gasps, Dan tells them that the police are after him. "I got out—the back door—as they were yelling at my wife—to let them in the front," he says. He looks at Ileana, his eyes pleading. "I knew you'd help me, Domnitza."

She glances at the others, brow furrowed in thought. They nod and start cleaning up the flour. There's no time to get to the castle, she thinks. Besides, there are already two others hiding there, who are in much greater danger than Dan. Nor can they hide him in the hospital. Finding him here would guarantee that the communists would shut it down.

She stares at the examining table as the others throw out ideas, gather bags, and tie the large bags of flour, then snaps her fingers. She turns to Dr. Puscariu.

"I know what! He has an intestinal obstruction. He needs an immediate operation!"

Puscariu's eyes light up and his teeth flash. The doctor, Ileana, and Sister Heidi, a nurse, dash out of the dispensary to the operating theater. As Sister Heidi throws the instruments into the sterilizer, Dan drops his clothes and puts on the hospital gown. Badillo prepares the ether, all of them glancing out of the windows for the police. In no time, Dan is on the table, lightly sedated, the others in position around him.

Dr. Puscariu glances at Ileana, on the other side of the table, the scalpel in his hand. She nods and he holds the sharp blade over Dan's stomach, intending only to break the skin.

But as the knife begins its journey, they hear the heavy tread in the hall, and voices from the waiting room. The scalpel pauses while they listen.

"We have information that Mr. Tomascu is here."

"Mr. Tomascu is not here." Dr. John's voice, steady and calm, comes from the hall. Sister Heidi wipes both Dr. Puscariu's and Ileana's foreheads to remove the sweat.

"He ran this way," insist the police. The voices are getting closer. Surely they won't barge into an operating theater?

"He did not come here," Dr. John says. "I've been here all afternoon and haven't seen him."

"We will search."

Puscariu looks piercingly at Ileana. She nods, and watches as his scalpel cuts deeper, through the skin, the fat, the muscle, into the peritoneum.

He looks at her again, brow wrinkled in a question. Ileana glances down, sees his hands around the mass of intestine and, grinning under the mask, she nods. Dr. Puscariu's eyes crinkle as he lifts out the pink, silver, and purple mass. It slithers and slides in fine, messy display.

The door bursts open, and Dr. John appears, face barely visible above the broad shoulders of two policemen.

Puscariu scowls at them and appears busy.

Ileana turns, and with insides quaking, uses her harshest voice. She hopes it convinces them. "What do you want? Get out of here at once. This is an operation in progress; do you want to kill the patient?"

Faces paling, the police look from her face to the mess on the operating room table. They gulp, shake their heads and back away, muttering what might be an apology. The door bangs shut, and a few moments later, Dan's insides are back where they belong as Ileana giggles a little hysterically in relief.

In spite of bizarre and sometimes funny incidents, the situation was so risky that Ileana supplied her family with suicide pills in case they were ever arrested. In 1946, Ileana came as close as she ever did to using one. After a supper at the castle one evening, Emile Bodnaras informed her that General Aldea had been captured and imprisoned. Bodnaras produced a written sheet that detailed everything Ileana had done for the underground. "I thanked God for the semi-obscurity, and kept my face in the shadow," she wrote. "I was also grateful for the long royal training that taught us to keep our feelings to ourselves . . . as I quietly and firmly denied everything. I hated myself for finding prudence the better part of valor, and for dissociating myself from my friend. I would have preferred to stand up beside him, but this would have been of no use to him and would have betrayed others who were concerned as well, and who had a right to my protection."

It was well known that no one escaped torture when they were arrested, and it was also known that the more important prisoners were shipped to the Soviet Union, where torture was even more "refined" and agonizing. It would be a major coup to be able to take a member of the royal family into custody—and Ileana would be treated even worse than others, simply because of her royal status. Had she not been able to lie as well as she did, it's likely the suicide pill would have been necessary.

In spite of the tension, life went on, and everyone adapted to the restrictions, shortages, and uncertainty of whom to trust. The women's and children's hospital wings were finished in the summer of 1946.

Most of the women had no one to look after their children while they were in hospital, so one section of the new wing was designated a day nursery for the children of in-patients. This may have been the first day-care center in Romania.

Ileana taught the women modern nutrition, hygiene, and child care. Isolated by the steep valleys, it was difficult for the women to learn about new ideas. But they picked up things quickly, which, to Ileana's immense satisfaction, resulted in a real improvement in health.

The staff organized a volleyball team, which played the village team. In winter, staff and family skied on the mountainous slopes. A popular glee club ran for several years and often did double duty as the church choir for feasts. Ileana gave the staff free run of the castle swimming pool, and everyone would troop up to a cold mountain pool where they swam and sunned in the summer.

By the spring of 1946, Ileana had created a daily schedule that let her work in the hospitals in the mornings and spend the afternoons with her family. She often combined this family time with necessary hospital work, as she made the rounds of villagers, or asked one or the other of her children to run errands. One summer, Minola and Sandi ran the children's ward under adult supervision.

Ileana returned to the hospital for the early evening, but was back home with Anton and the children for dinner and games. Monopoly and reading aloud were favorites, or, for the adults, bridge. With six children, there was often rough-housing in the castle, and Ileana laughed at the thought that future visitors to Bran might assume the gouges in the stone walls were due to some pitched battle fought in days gone by, when in fact they'd been made by the go-carts her children raced down the stairs!

In July of 1946, Anton encouraged Ileana to take the three older children and visit a friend who lived in the Oltania valley, along the Olt River. She did, and in spite of the drought, which was in its second summer, had a wonderful rest. They rambled over the area, saw the monastery where she and her Guides had stayed, swam in the Olt River, and visited, for the first time, the gravesites of her family—of her parents, King Ferdinand, who'd died before the children were born, and of their beloved grandmother, Queen Marie.

When Ileana returned, Bodnaras encouraged her to apply for Anton's freedom, and, as if to cement their renewed good relations, King Mihai lent his support to the application.

Life, with the changes due to the effects of the war and the increasing tension under the communist regime, did continue, but those changes were the harbinger of worse to come.

CHAPTER TWENTY

Exile

Weep bitterly for him who goes away, for he shall return no more
to see his native land. (Jeremiah 22:10)

ife under the communists grew harder and more tense. With the shortages, devastation, and upheaval of war still evident in every aspect of life, obtaining even normal household supplies was a challenge. Many medical supplies, like rubber gloves and sheets or specialized surgical instruments, were unobtainable.

The government put pressure on officials at all levels to prove that life under communism was perfect. Ileana discovered that this mentality persisted even at the cost of life itself.

In the fall of 1946, a typhoid epidemic broke out around Bran and spread quickly in the drought-stricken area. Because of the demand for perfection, Ileana couldn't get the local officials to admit an epidemic existed. Were they to admit there was a problem, they would be blamed, even for an epidemic. Arrests would be quick, and the officials would never be heard from again. It wasn't until she appealed directly to the minister of health in person that Ileana got the help the region so desperately needed.

As if this wasn't enough, Ileana's back condition worsened. Since the accident on her boat, the *Isprava*, in the late 1920s, she had been plagued with problems and frequent pain. Now, at thirty-seven, because of the strenuous work of lifting patients, shoveling snow, and pushing cars, she was in severe pain most of the time and her mobility was limited. She was treated in Bucharest, but not very successfully. She did what she could to carry on as normally as possible, to the limits of her pain.

Between epidemics, back treatments, and hiding public enemies, Ileana had maintained the pressure for Anton's release, which finally came through late in the fall. He left almost immediately for Soviet-occupied Austria to see what could be salvaged from their old home in Sonnberg.

Christmas that year, even without Anton, was "a happy one." Ileana reported, "When I say 'happy' I mean it in the modified sense we were becoming accustomed to. We had no critical cases at the hospital at the time, no major disaster overtook us, and the winter was not so severe as the one we had had the year before. The Turku Canal, which supplied our electric current, lacked water, so that we were often reduced to oil lamps. I rather liked this at home, but it was a serious problem in the hospital."

Anton returned unsuccessful from his attempt to travel to Sonnberg, but he'd applied for permission to enter the country, and it was a matter of waiting until it came through.

Shortly after the New Year, Ileana was selected as head of one of the teams designated to distribute a huge shipment of food donated by President Truman of the United States. She requested the region of Piatra-Neamtz, in the northwest of Moldavia, where she had spent the wonderful summer at Bicaz in 1918. In March, she, Mrs. Podgoreanu from the Brasov Red Cross canteen, and twelve others traveled by train to the region.

As well as feeling elated that she could help alleviate some of the hunger, Ileana was delighted to return to a place that held such memories—and overjoyed to find the people remembered her. "*Domnitza, nu'tzi amintesti?*" "Your Highness, do you not remember?" "There was hardly a village, a monastery or a convent which I visited where I was not greeted by these words," she wrote.

The trip was a success, both for the morale of the Romanians and for America's reputation, but also in a way no one had foreseen. Among the food packages were bags of peas. Rather than eat them, the people planted some and waited for them to sprout. When they did, the peas were put carefully away. It was the only seed crop available, and it meant at least one harvest for the year.

When the Communist Party realized how popular the Americans had become, they shut down the few remaining relief organizations or cut them off from their international connections. In spite of Ileana's spirited and impassioned defense, the first organization to go was her beloved Red Cross.

By the end of the summer, the handwriting on the wall was clear—and not just for the relief organizations. Earlier, the communists had not dared remove King Mihai. He was popular and carried enough power that to depose him would bring revolt, led by the heroes of past wars and of previous governments.

His position, her relationship to him, and her own popularity with the people lent Ileana and her family some protection. In addition, she had proved over and over again that she was no "parasite" on the people's backs, but rather gave health, healing, and comfort to those around her.

By 1947, most of the non-communist leaders had been arrested, killed, or terrorized into silence. The common people lived in abject fear, knowing they could be arrested for anything at any time. Ileana knew it wouldn't be long before they found an excuse to remove her.

There was nothing she could do, so she continued as she had begun—treating her people and living her life. But she thought about escape, even daydreaming about it during a family holiday to Constanza. She knew it was a dream—she couldn't leave Romania.

After the holiday, Anton received permission to travel to Austria and returned in December, just in time for Christmas. He was laden with presents for the family and precious supplies for the hospital. As a special celebration, Ileana took the diamond-and-sapphire diadem out of the safe and wore it on Christmas Day.

The next days were peaceful—the family drove to Sinaia to visit Mihai and his mother, and on the evening of the thirtieth, Ileana visited her longtime friend Iona.

On her return, she was greeted by the terrified caretaker, who told her that Mihai had been forced to abdicate.

Frightened, unsure of what was coming, Ileana drove to Bucharest. Only a day or so later, officials arrived at her door and told her that she and her family could leave the country, taking with them only what they could carry, or . . . they could be confined in a monastery until they were executed.

She and Anton chose to leave, and the last frenzied days were spent packing the house in Bucharest. When she returned to Bran, she discovered that the castle had been sealed until her return. The family had twenty-four hours to pack under supervision. The guards secured each suitcase with a wire lock, for fear the family would "steal" the "people's" treasures.

Ileana discovered the jeweled diadem, which they hadn't replaced in the safe. Anton and Stefan arranged a slight distraction for the guards, and while she hurriedly wrapped the diadem in a nightgown, Stefan pulled the hinge pins from the back of one of the suitcases and they slipped the tiara in. Stefan quickly closed the case and replaced the pins with the guards none the wiser.

Ileana took a few moments to visit her brother's grave, which she had moved in 1940 after an earthquake damaged Cotroceni Palace, where Mircea was originally buried. Then she crossed from the castle to her mother's shrine. "Anton, the children, and I knelt for the last time at the shrine of the heart, praying deeply and silently. . . . From one of the tables in the castle I had taken a lovely old metal box, and pushing aside the snow with my hands, I filled it with Romanian soil. This, of all I carried away with me, is the most precious thing I have."

She wept with the hospital patients and the household servants, then returned to the gatehouse and said goodbye to her staff.

"I've often wondered," she said, "if you have time before you die, if you would look round that same way as I did when I left and thought to myself, this I shall see no more. This is an end, this and this and you touch things and you talk to people, and you say goodbye, but you have not the relief of parting with your body as well. You have to take that with you, and that is what is so terribly difficult: is to take yourself along."

They climbed into the car and drove away, getting stuck in a muddy field in Tohan as they tried to avoid the snow-drifted roads. The town was considered totally "red," completely given over to communism, and when Ileana asked some of the workmen from the factory—the factory that had donated an entire operating theater to her hospital, whose workers she had treated free of charge for over four years—for help, they complied in sullen silence. She returned to the car for her purse, and then, against the advice of the guards, retraced her steps to the little knot of taciturn men.

Ileana Remembers

"Thank you," I said to them. "Please take this and divide it among you. I know it is little, but it is all I have." And I held out to them what money had been left to me.

The men looked at one another, and then one stepped out from among them.

"No, Domnitza," he said to me sorrowfully. "No, Domnitza, not today will we take a gift from you. Have you not been at our beck and call night and day? None has knocked at your door without being received. We have rendered you so small but so sad a service—see, the very earth is loath to let you go! But one request we still have of you. Will you kneel down with us and say a prayer for King and country, and for your return?"

And there, in that muddy field, as the sun slowly set behind the Carpathians and filled the world with a last glow of splendor, I knelt down, joining in prayer with the factory workmen and those who till the soil. "Our Father, Who art in heaven . . ."

Above: Princess Ileana visiting Philadelphia

Facing page: Princess Ileana testifying before the Committee on Communist Aggression as to her personal experiences when the communists entered Romania

Section V

Heimatlos

TIMELINE 1948–1966

YEAR	COUNTRY	EVENT
1948	Argentina	Ileana and family move from Switzerland to Argentina: Ileana is 39, Anton 48, Stefan almost 15, Marie (Minola) 15, Alexandra 12, Maria Magdalena 9, and Elizabeth (Herzi) 6
	Britain	Prince Charles, eldest son of Princess Elizabeth & Prince Phillip, born
1950	USA	Ileana arrives in Boston, Massachusetts, for medical treatment; Anton returns to Austria
	USA	McCarthy elected, Red Scare begins
	Korea	Korean War begins—involves UN member nations
1952	USA	Congress passes special bill to allow Ileana & her children to remain in the US
	Canada	Vincent Massey first Canadian-born governor general
	USA	Dwight D. Eisenhower elected president
	Britain	King George VI dies; succeeded by Queen Elizabeth II
1953	USA	Ileana continues lecturing on the evils of communism and the fate of Romania
	Portugal	Deposed King Carol II (Ileana's brother) dies at age 60
	Britain	First publication of description of DNA molecule
	Korea	Korean War ends
1954	USA	Ileana divorces Anton; marries Stefan Issarescu; Stefan Habsburg (Ileana's son) marries Jerrine Soper
	USA	McCarthy discredited, end of Red Scare
	Britain	*Lord of the Rings* published
1956	France	Elisabeta (Ileana's sister) dies at age 62
1957	USA	Ileana undergoes surgery for her back; Ileana's first grandchild, Christopher, born
	Austria	Maria Ileana (Minola) marries Jaroslav "Rus" Kottulinsky
1958	USA, Austria	Ileana's grandchildren born—Maria Ileana (Minola's child, Austria) and Ileana Habsburg (Stefan's child, USA)
1959	South America	Maria Ileana (Minola) killed in plane crash

YEAR	COUNTRY	EVENT
1959	USA	Stefan dangerously ill with encephalitis; Peter Habsburg (Stefan's child) born
	Austria	Maria Magdalena (Magi) marries Baron Hans Ulrich von Holzhausen
1960	USA	Ileana's son Dominic (Niki) marries Engle von Voss; Constanza (Stefan's child) born
	Austria	Johannes (Magi's first child) born
1961	France	Ileana joins the monastery in Bussy-en-Othe, France, to test vocation
	England	Marie (Mignon), Ileana's sister, dies at age 61
1962	Austria	Alexandra (Sandi) marries; Georg (Magi's child) born
	USA	John Glenn first man to orbit the earth; Cuban Missile Crisis; military advisors sent to Vietnam
	Canada	Launch of Alouette 1, space satellite
1963	Austria	Alexandra (Magi's child) stillborn
	Britain	US, UK & USSR sign nuclear test ban treaty
	USA	JFK assassinated; Lyndon Johnson becomes president
	Canada	Lester B. Pearson elected prime minister
1964	Austria	Elisabeth (Herzi) marries
	USA	Anton (Stefan's son) born; beginning of search for location of the American monastery
	Canada	Canada adopts new flag
	USA	Lyndon Johnson elected president
	Britain	Death penalty abolished
1965	France	Ileana divorces Stefan Issarescu; takes first vows as monastic at Bussy
	Austria	Sandor (Niki's son) born
	Britain	Winston Churchill dies at age 90
1966	Austria	Anton (Herzi's son) born
	Canada	First ever attempt to blow up House of Commons
	Britain	Tension with Rhodesia; anti-Vietnam War protests; Beatles play last live concert
	USA	Miranda rights established; NOW formed; anti-Vietnam & civil rights protests continue

CHAPTER TWENTY-ONE

Living Death

My grief is beyond healing, my heart is sick within me.
(Jeremiah 8:18, NKJV)

leana moved through the next years looking after the children, discussing prospects and the future with Anton and helping her fellow refugees, but inside herself, she was "as one dead."

Imagine This

Ileana stands in her icon corner, eyes fixed on the Mother of God, who holds the somber-faced Infant on her knee. She begins the prayers. "Glory to the Father, and to the Son, and to the Holy Spirit, now and ever and unto ages of ages, amen. O Lord, have mercy on me, a sinner. O Lord, have mercy on me . . ."

The words continue, but they're just words. They come from her mind, out of her mouth, empty of the love, the dedication, the joy she'd always felt when praying before. Once the formal prayers are said, she stands, unable to open her heart as she has in the past and pour out her feelings and thoughts. There are no words to express what she feels, for most of the time, she feels nothing at all. All is dead inside.

She considers the emptiness and tests it again. What if her children were taken from her? She shrugs. It would be awful, and she would miss them, their voices, their hugs, their laughter and tears, but she can summon none of the sorrow, the panic, and the devastation such thoughts caused even as little as two years ago.

She should finish and leave—there's so much to be done, but something holds her in place, and she shifts her gaze to the icon of the Lord Himself—His eyes as compassionate and sorrowful as always.

As she stands, she feels a pressure around her—not physical, exactly, but what it is she can't say. It holds her gently in place, saying the things she cannot say for herself.

As she gazes at the icon of the Lord, she realizes that this is the Church—the prayers of the faithful, of the monastics who stand for hours and days before their icons. They are saying for her the words she cannot think, expressing the feelings she cannot feel, keeping her standing, keeping her heart open, empty and waiting. She nods, not content, exactly, and not feeling anything more than she has since the night her family left Romania, but not ready yet to leave the corner and God's and the Church's embrace. If she cannot pray, then she will let the Church pray for her, until the words come back.

IT WAS AN ENORMOUS EFFORT FOR ILEANA to move through her life. Not only was she unable to pray, and not only were her material circumstances hard to bear, but so was "the need to live at all. I did not doubt for a moment the . . . necessity of my presence for my six children; my love for them was as strong and potent as ever. But inside, . . . the essential me upon which all the rest is built—suffered a mortal shock when my life was severed from my people."

The family settled first in Switzerland, where a friend had also fled. Stefan Tsoculescu was a wealthy businessman who had donated generously to her hospital. Before the exile, when he'd been arrested by the communists, Ileana had used her influence with high-ranking party official Emile Bodnaras to have him freed. Once exiled, they met him in Switzerland, where he interested Anton in a business venture. He persuaded Ileana to finance it by mortgaging and pawning most of the jewelry she had brought with her, including the sapphire-and-diamond tiara, as well as using whatever funds she could free from frozen assets outside Romania.

When they discovered that they couldn't work in Switzerland, they agreed that Argentina would be the best place to begin the new company, which was to manufacture electrical cable. Argentina was also the only country that would accept Ileana's family—now commoners, their surname now Habsburg. They had been declared public enemies by the communists, both Russian and Romanian, and there was a price on her head— no country wanted to risk letting them in.

Enough money was released to her to enable her to pay for her family's trip, and they arrived in Argentina in the summer of 1948.

It wasn't long before Ileana discovered that Tsoculescu's company was a front for the black market and for right-wing, hard-line Romanian politics. She quickly severed any connection with the company, enraging Tsoculescu, who vowed he would ruin her. She fought for two years to get her money out of the company he ran, but ended up losing about $75,000 (over a million dollars in today's currency). Tsoculescu was able to foster and pass on a number of rumors and lies about Ileana's involvement with the Nazis and the Iron Guard of Romania, and he revived the stories of her collaboration with the communists. There were even rumors that she'd taken lovers high in the communist government.

A large number of Romanian refugees wound up in Argentina, and the conditions under which they were living were deplorable. Ileana and a priest she knew as Father Dan worked to get a home for her fellow exiles, visited them, and helped them get back on their feet.

Argentina suited neither Ileana nor Anton—she reported to a friend that quality medical help could only be obtained "for show or money." She said that "two years under Peron in Argentina, . . . were more difficult than even the four years under the Communists and the six years under the Nazis."

Besides the continuing efforts for the Romanian people in exile, Ileana worked for her children's education. By September of 1949, through the efforts of Bishop O'Hara, whom she had known in Romania, and Julie Thompson, a woman who had worked in Romania in the days before Queen Marie died, Stefan and Minola were enrolled on scholarship in prep schools in the United States.

Ileana's financial troubles, already bad because of her frozen assets and her ongoing struggle with Stefan Tsoculescu, worsened in 1949, when her brother-in-law began a lawsuit against her. This froze the little money she had available, and she was almost destitute again.

If these troubles weren't enough, her health gave out almost completely—her back, which had been under treatment in Romania, worsened, and she had stomach, liver, and digestive problems that resulted in repeated hospitalizations and bed rest. She was also emotionally bankrupt, and at one point, as she related in a letter to Julie Thompson, she was fainting up to five times a day, for no apparent reason. She couldn't drive and was forced to put off necessary work for the family.

Her letters at the time indicate her total impatience with her illnesses, and she relates that she feels "very humiliated that a daughter of my Mother's could be such a weakling."

Ileana had trouble with insomnia, and when she did manage to sleep, she suffered from nightmares in which she wandered as a ghost through a wintry Romania filled with savage and terrified strangers. She also experienced a return of the 1919 nightmares of the horrors of Jassy, and worse ones of demons and hell. The only respite was to make the sign of the cross in her dreams, and upon waking to turn to an icon of her guardian angel. "I knew positively as I did when I saw him," she wrote, "that he was standing by me to protect me."[3] At peace, she would fall asleep and rest without dreams.

In the years between 1938 and 1948, Ileana and Anton had spent very little time together. Ileana had tried to meet Anton whenever he had leave, but as the war dragged on it became more and more difficult to travel. They were reunited in 1944, but the three years of house arrest under the communist regime were full of terror and uncertainty. The ongoing stress of the exile, the disastrous business venture, and Ileana's breakdown were further pressures on an already troubled marriage.

Anton wanted to return to Austria—his citizenship had been restored after the war, and he hoped to salvage the estate at Sonnberg, which was in the Soviet occupation zone. Ileana had had enough of communism to last her a lifetime.

CHAPTER TWENTY-TWO

Healing & Growth

For with the Lord there is mercy,
And with Him is abundant redemption.
(Psalm 129:7)

Ileana Remembers

There is one thing I cannot show you: one very important thing which I was allowed to bring with me from my old life, and which made the foundation of my new one. You can see it in a photograph of my mother . . . but no picture can give you any idea of the living glow and the rainbow fires in the sapphire and diamond tiara she is wearing.

The tiara and I both entered the United States . . . 1950, when I flew from Argentina to Miami—hoping to avoid any public recognition—with the tiara wrapped in my nightgown!

Because by this time I was suffering severely from arthritis, I received permission in May, 1950, to come to the United States for medical treatment. As I gathered all my forces, physical and financial, to make this trip, I felt desperately that I was nearing the end of my endurance. I pawned everything I had of value in order to leave my family in Buenos Aires the money to live on . . . I could not afford to insure something whose "breakup" value had once been appraised at eighty thousand dollars, so I decided to wrap it in my nightgown and keep it with me in a small bag. Thus with *three hundred dollars, a ticket to Boston, and a hidden tiara, I prepared to enter the United States. . . .*

Anxious, weary, in pain, but strangely hopeful, I finally arrived in Miami, where the long flight was interrupted. I lined up for customs inspection, glad to see that no word of my arrival had preceded me on this . . . entrance into the United States. I had not realized how public the inspection would be, and when it was my turn and I answered that I had something to declare, I asked if I could unpack my bag in private. The officer was good humored, but a little impatient with my hesitation. When I insisted on it, he made it clear that he thought I was being a nuisance.

"What have you got there, anyway—a corpse?" he asked me.

However, when he finally led me to an office and I opened my bag, it was my turn to feel a little superior. It was obvious that he did not know quite what to do when a tiara turned up in the luggage he inspected. He touched the central sapphire a little gingerly. Since it weighed 125 carats it was nearly the size of a man's pocket watch. Was it real? he wanted to know. When I assured him that it was, he looked still more harassed, but finally he decided that he would send it to Boston "in bond." Together we wrapped it in a newspaper and put it into a box, which he duly sealed and ticketed. It was with a qualm, I confess, that I watched it put into the luggage compartment of the plane for Boston before I myself embarked. If it should somehow be lost, I was losing everything I had, and it was now out of my hands!

Arriving in Boston, I was told that, since it was Sunday, all offices were

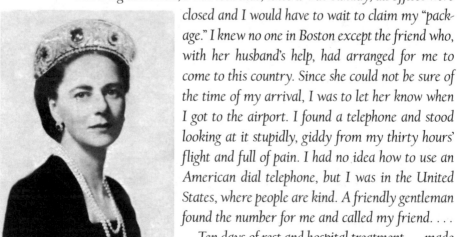

closed and I would have to wait to claim my "package." I knew no one in Boston except the friend who, with her husband's help, had arranged for me to come to this country. Since she could not be sure of the time of my arrival, I was to let her know when I got to the airport. I found a telephone and stood looking at it stupidly, giddy from my thirty hours' flight and full of pain. I had no idea how to use an American dial telephone, but I was in the United States, where people are kind. A friendly gentleman found the number for me and called my friend. . . .

Ten days of rest and hospital treatment . . . made

me able to find my way to the customhouse and inquire for my "parcel." It took some time for the officials to trace it, and I felt some stabs of alarm until it was finally located in a safe in another building. But even within sight of it there was a further delay—I must get a "customhouse broker"! I had never heard of such a thing, and when it was explained to me I naturally asked:

"But whom shall I get?"

"Oh, we are not allowed to recommend any particular broker, but there are plenty around here," replied one of the gentlemen, waving his hand casually in the direction of the window. I looked out, and my eye fell on a sign across the street: "Stone & Downer, Custom House Brokers." Why not go there? I thought to myself—so I did!

Everyone was very matter of fact about the whole thing, both then and the next day, when we all met by appointment in an office of the customhouse on Atlantic Avenue. Everyone was very matter of fact until the parcel was opened, and the officials saw what had been lying about the office for ten days—for even I, who was so familiar with it, felt always a thrill of delight at the radiance of blue and white fire when the tiara was suddenly brought into the light. The faces of the men revealed their shocked amazement. They gasped. Then one smiled, relieved.

"But of course you have this insured!" he said.

"Oh, no," I told him calmly. "Why should I? It has escaped the Nazis and the Communists safely. Naturally I did not expect to lose it here!"

They were evidently uncertain whether to laugh or to scold me, but from that moment we were all friends. One of the men asked me to autograph a visitors' register he kept—"with all your titles and things!" he explained; and I was tempted to draw him a little sketch of the tiara as a souvenir. The age of the jewel was found to make it free of customs, so eventually I walked off with it under my arm—still in its somewhat battered cardboard box. When it was rewrapped with the help of Mr. Irvine, who represented my "Custom House Brokers," I tucked it under my arm again and walked up State Street to the post office, where I mailed the package to a jeweler in New York. That was not its last journey. Sometimes it was guarded by police, at other times my son carried it about in the subway! Finally, after much trouble, worry, and heartbreak, it was sold for a sum *much below its value. It was both beautiful and splendid, but my children were in need. As it stood, it neither fed us nor clothed us nor warmed us. I could not even wear it!*

THE REMAINING CHILDREN—Sandi, Niki, Magi, and Herzi—came to the US on the funds from the diadem. Ileana enrolled them in school and put a down payment on a house in Newton, Massachusetts. She purchased furniture from Goodwill, and bought eating utensils and a cookbook at the local five-and-dime.

Anton returned permanently to Austria.

In spite of her recovery, the connections with Romanian friends, and her family's safety, Ileana was bitterly lonely. No one, she felt, could share her experience. Her life had been cut in two. She was at the peak of her powers, in what she believed to be the fullest and most creative period of her life, and all of her accomplishments, physical, intellectual, and spiritual, had been "wiped off the face of the earth as a sponge washes off a blackboard."

"I do not know," she wrote, "if you can imagine what it is like to part from all you have loved and known, and to start again without being able to share memories of the past with any one of those you live with. . . . It is sad not to be able to turn around and say to someone, "Do you remember . . . ?"

There was guilt as well, which was something no one could understand. She had left her people, who couldn't escape from the terrifying regime. In spite of knowing she would have died had she remained, and that she could do far more alive in exile than dead in Romania, the feeling of failure, of having abandoned her country and her people, remained with her. She never forgot those who could not escape, and much of her work was done for them. "I owe something," she said, "to those who've remained behind, and those who resist because the wonderful part is they do go on resisting."

Only by turning completely to God did she find the pain easing, and she more and more found herself praying, sometimes wordlessly, sometimes in silent anguish, sometimes with tears. Sometimes, she just stood in her icon corner, upheld by the prayers of the Church and the angels.

Photos taken of Ileana during the 1950s show her anguish clearly if one knows how to look. While the beautiful woman with the composed, serene face is clearly Ileana Habsburg, Princess of Romania, there is a melancholy laid deep in her eyes, a heaviness of spirit and a sorrow that informs everything about the woman in the picture. Photographs of Ileana taken in the 1950s have much of the same solemnity as those taken during World War I.

A co-worker she'd known in Romania took her to a house in Louisburg Square in Boston and introduced her to the Sisters of St. Margaret, an Episcopal order of nuns. "I knew I had found my spiritual home," said Ileana of the convent. She visited the nuns more and more often, feeling "less like a wandering spirit, but more as one who returns."

Shortly after she and the children had settled, Ileana accepted a speaking invitation for which she was astounded to earn twenty-five dollars. She realized that she could get into trouble for this, since she and her children had entered the US on temporary permits. When her treatment and their schooling were finished, they were supposed to leave. But Congress passed a special bill, introduced by Senator John F. Kennedy, that enabled

Byerly-Kaupp Photography

Ileana with Archbishop Valerian and ladies of ARFORA (a Romanian Orthodox women's group)

Ileana to remain and work in the US. She accepted more speaking engagements all over the country, estimating at one point that she'd traveled over 60,000 miles in one year alone. Since all the children were in boarding school, she was free to travel as much as she needed, as it meant money to pay the bills, and her arthritis no longer allowed her to work as a nurse. The speaking tours also meant that she could spread the word about communism and its effects in Romania, as well as solicit help for those left behind.

She wrote her memoirs, *I Live Again*, in 1952, dedicated to those "brave souls that have remained behind," and *Hospital of the Queen's Heart*, about the Bran facility, in 1953.

The years 1954 to 1960 saw a new phase in Ileana's life. Her children were growing up. Stefan was 22 in 1954, Minola 21, Sandi 19, Niki 17, Magi 15, and Herzi 12. Most of them were moving into independent, adult lives of their own, which freed Ileana to extend her lecturing and begin new activity with the Romanian Orthodox Church.

In June of 1954, after divorcing Anton, Ileana accepted a marriage proposal from her good friend, Stefan Issarescu, a doctor who specialized in pathology and was a pioneer in atomic medical research.

Also that year, her son Stefan married Mary Jerrine Soper, at St. Elizabeth's Episcopal Church in nearby Milton, Massachusetts.

Ileana had reached a new peace. She was coming to terms with her exile, and realized that even here, through God's good grace, she could still help her people. Even though she was newly married, she still felt the yearning toward the peace and solitude of the monastic life, and began to explore it more deeply. She recorded addresses for the Voice of America and spoke on Radio Free Europe, sending messages of hope and freedom, as well as daily meditations and Bible readings, to her captive people. As her income increased and her assets became available, she used some of the money to smuggle goods and small luxuries into Romania for those who were left behind.

Her daughters, as they finished school, returned to Austria, began their careers, and married. Niki finished his architect's training at the Rhode Island School of Design.

In 1957, Stefan and his wife Jerri presented Ileana with her first grandchild, Christopher, and in Austria, Minola, now 24, married Jaroslav Kottulinsky, whom the family called Rus.

While the medical treatment in 1950 had gone a long way to relieve the constant pain Ileana lived in, by 1957 the arthritis had gotten so bad she had to have a cervical laminectomy to relieve the pressure on her spinal cord and nerves. Because it was spinal surgery, with possibly serious complications, she had to remain still and in bed for several weeks after the operation while she healed.

During the enforced idleness, Ileana reflected on her life. Her children were mostly grown. Herzi, the youngest of the children, was now 15. Ileana's new marriage, in spite of her best efforts, was not going well, and she had come to the conclusion that she'd made a serious mistake. She now had more independence and freedom to do as she wished. She longed to spend more time with God in prayer and quiet, where she could listen to His voice and pray to Him with no interruptions or demands from the world.

When she recovered, she began teaching at the Vatra* summer camps of the Romanian Orthodox Episcopate near Grass Lake, Michigan. Here she learned how little the American Romanians remembered about their homeland and their religious and monastic heritage.

Ileana was serious enough about her desire for the monastic life to speak with both Stefan and her husband about it. Stefan and Jerri were supportive and encouraged her to at least explore the possibility, but according to her son, Ileana's husband disapproved.

The year 1959 brought sorrow back into Ileana's life. She had made some deep and lasting friends in America, her children were obviously thriving in the peaceful, prosperous country, and over the past ten years she had managed to come to terms with her exile. While not happy years, they had been peaceful years of healing and a growing contentment. During this time the isolation had eased, but in January, just days after her fiftieth birthday, tragedy struck.

Minola, pregnant with her second child, was accompanying her husband to South America. As the plane descended toward the airport runway in Rio de Janeiro, it crashed, killing everyone aboard.

"Why? Many have asked me, should she who was so beautiful, so young, so happy, be killed? . . . in that terrible hour . . . came the news that both Minola and her husband, Rus, had been killed in an aircrash, I felt a searing, unutterable pain. It was as if the blood had drained from my heart and my body had been torn asunder." But, as devastated as she was, Ileana clung to God. "There is no painless consolation for this bereavement . . . The best and only way is for me to face the stark reality and to look at it with Christian courage—seeking to see the light and truth not *around* my grief, but *through* it. My child has stepped over the threshold into life eternal; this I know beyond the shadow of a doubt."

As if one disaster wasn't enough, that summer, Stefan came down with a severe case of viral encephalitis. Once he was released from the hospital, he needed round-the-clock nursing, and at Ileana's insistence, his whole family moved for six months into the Newton house. Once Stefan was better and could return to his own home, Ileana wasted no time—she went to her bishop about a possible monastic vocation.

CHAPTER TWENTY-THREE

Sister Ileana

These all continued with one accord in prayer and supplication. (Acts 1:14)

t's recommended that those who are contemplating the monastic life stay for a while in a monastery, both to test their call and to find a monastery they will suit and that will suit them. In the 1950s and '60s, there were very few monasteries in North America. Of those that did exist, none were Romanian, none were English-language based, and very few, if any, were for women. Ileana would have to return to Europe to test her call.

His Grace, Bishop Anthony Bloom, suggested she visit the Monastery of the Protection of the Veil of the Mother of God, in Bussy-en-Othe in France.

⊰⊱⊰⊱⊰⊱ Imagine This ⊰⊱⊰⊱⊰⊱

The nun sets the bags down by the bed.

"Dinner is at five," she says in French. "If you wish to sleep through, do so. We know you've had a long trip and are tired. Vespers and evening prayers are immediately after dinner, if you care to join us. But sleep first. Mother Eudoxia will see you tomorrow morning. Sleep well." The nun nods to Ileana, closing the door quietly behind her. Ileana sits on the bed, weary but peaceful, soaking in the serenity of the monastery.

Located in a valley, the monastery is housed in an ancient manor house and its grounds. The cloisters are in the manor house, the chapel is a converted stable, and the guesthouse rooms look toward the garden, still covered in snow this early in the year. Ileana gazes out the window, runs her hand along the bedspread.

Although she'll never again see her beloved Romania, the quiet hush is exactly like that in the monasteries back home, and Ileana feels a peace that has eluded her for years sinking into her bones and muscles.

She'd dreamed of this, in Austria when the children were small, and now she's here. She gazes at the snow-covered plants, the neat plots outlined by the swept walk. She wants to see the flowers thrust through the wet, thawed ground, watch them grow, mature, bloom, and die, to be replaced by the summer blossoms, and then by the blanket of snow next winter and the next and the one after that.

She never wants to leave, and with a burst of contented joy realizes that if she and the mothers suit each other, she will never have to. She can stay here for the rest of her life, praying and praising God. Impulsively, she turns to the icon, crossing herself and offering a quick, heartfelt prayer of thanks for the mercy God has always shown her.

WHILE THE MONASTERY BECAME HER HOME, Ileana couldn't stay there year round. In order to maintain her permanent residency status, she needed to live for a certain length of time each year in the US. As in the days of her unofficial exile under King Carol's rule, when she shuttled between Romania and Austria, now Ileana spent her time traveling between France and the US, where she continued to teach at the Vatra about monasticism and Orthodoxy.

As the time of her formal admission to monasticism approached, Ileana had to tie up the loose ends of her secular life—one of which was legally ending her second marriage.

She took up residence in Nevada for six months, as their law required, before she could get a divorce. While there, she worked at an Indian reservation. The poverty of the people touched her, and the land itself

Sister Ileana at the monastery at Bussy

appealed to her—the desert was where monasticism began, after all.

But from the first week of Lent, 1961, when she was fifty-two years of age, the converted manor house at Bussy-en-Othe became Ileana's home.

There were many questions from her friends and supporters, and she addressed these in an open letter published in 1961. "I have now entered the monastic life," she wrote, "because I felt and feel, without the shadow of doubt, that this is the one and only right way for me from now on."

While some aspects of life as a nun came easily to Ileana—now Sister Ileana—there were difficulties as well. The most obvious and hardest to overcome was the language barrier. Ileana had been speaking French most of her life. But she had no understanding of Slavonic, which was the liturgical language of the monastery. Fortunately, one of the nuns, Mother Mary, was fluent in both English and Slavonic, and offered to translate the services for Sister Ileana.

Another difficulty must have been living with the other monastics. Private rooms are not a feature of life in a European monastery, and the nuns would be in each other's company almost continually. As one monastic explained, "It's like living with [several] of your not-so-closest friends."

The nuns rose together, prayed together, ate together, worked together. But living in a monastic community isn't a normal "in the world" relationship. "The past has to be put aside, and the novice is like a newborn in the spiritual life of the community, taking the lowest and last place," said another monastic. The purpose is to die to self, to focus on Christ and to pay attention only to Him.

The nuns came from different backgrounds—from royalty, as in Sister Ileana's case, to women who had never known anything as luxurious as a bed with sheets or a table with cutlery. For someone raised as royalty, and with a personality that needed solitude and quiet, it must have been a difficult adjustment.

The submission to authority was less of a problem for her—her parents had trained her all her life to submit to her royal duty. Monastic submission was just a different kind of duty. Even so, it must have been hard to ask for a blessing for something as simple as a walk in the garden or to clean up a spill.

In spite of this, she was able to form close connections with the other nuns and to learn from them—from the humility of Mother Martha, to the lessons in monastic love from Mother Joan, and the traditions of monastic discipline from Mother Theodosia.

In spite of the difficulties, however, Ileana found a deep and abiding joy—the same joy that every monastic speaks of. The joy of learning to submit to God's will, of staying in constant and prayerful awareness of His presence, was a balm that overlaid everything.

Ileana lived with the nuns and tested both her vocation and her fit with the monastery at Bussy-en-Othe. As Stefan wrote, "After about a year as a postulant, Jerri and I visited her in France. . . . She was more at peace than I had seen her in a long time."

Imagine This

Ileana mounts the stairs slowly, nodding to the other nuns as she and Mother Eudoxia pass them. It's free time, and the sisters are allowed to occupy themselves however they wish for a couple of hours. As soon as they reach the landing, their steps quicken, and the two middle-aged women hurry up the last flight. They scamper down the hall, burst through a door and shut it behind them, giggling like schoolgirls.

Ileana takes the fruit from her pockets as Mother Eudoxia selects a record and puts it on. They sit by the window, soaking in the warm spring sun and the music as the orchestra swells to George Enescu's *Romanian Rhapsody*.

"Ah, that is so good!" Mother Eudoxia says as the last strains die away. "It is such a nice treat, to listen to such wonderful music." Mother Eudoxia settles herself more comfortably on the window seat and looks over at Sister Ileana.

Sister Ileana nods as she takes an apple from the bowl. "Yes. I don't miss much from the world except my symphonies and operas."

They don't come up here often, but once in a while, Mother Eudoxia's eyes will gleam in a certain way, she'll nod toward the stairs, and when their free time comes, she and Sister Ileana will sneak away.

Mother Eudoxia bites into a grape. "Have you thought any more about America? Are you still convinced that is where God wants you to go?"

Sister Ileana nods. "The more I go back, the more certain I am. People aren't at all aware of the spiritual treasures of Orthodoxy, or of our monastic tradition. When I teach at the Vatra in the summer, they beg for more teaching on prayer, for the traditions that we've known all our lives. I am so blessed, so fortunate."

"How so?" asks Mother Eudoxia.

"I have the traditions that keep me anchored in my faith. I've grown up with them and I carry them wherever I go. They exiled me, they took away my country and my people. You know how lost I was, I told you all about it."

Mother Eudoxia nods. "And I know you still grieve for it, even now."

Sister Ileana bows her head, and says in a low voice, "I know, I'm sorry. I try not to hurt so much, but . . ."

"No, that hurt will never go away, not as long as you can't return." Mother reaches out and squeezes Ileana's hand. "But we are all exiled, and perhaps God is giving you a stronger taste of being a stranger in a strange land. Our true home is heaven, and it's been given to you to know, more than most of us, how that feels."

"You always know how to turn a sorrow into a blessing, Matushka. You're like my own mother, and I feel I can trust you as much as I did her, to know my heart and to say the one thing that will bring me comfort." Ileana smiles and they listen for a little while to the music, enjoying the sun's warmth as the light floods into the room.

Finally Ileana speaks again. "You and I, we grew up with our faith, with the traditions and the habits from childhood. We carry it with us wherever we go." Mother nods as Ileana continues, "The people in America, their grandparents and great-grandparents came with the same traditions, but now, those are just folk tales they tell their children. They hunger for something deeper, some way of bringing their faith and their relationship with God more completely into the bones of their lives. I think He's calling me to help them. By opening a monastery in America, I can bring those traditions back, and give them some of the peace that the monasteries and the closeness to God have always given us."

Mother nods and checks her watch. "We can't stay here much longer—free time is almost up. But we'll talk more later. What do you want to hear next?"

"Oh, you know, I would love to hear some Rachmaninoff!"

Both Mother Eudoxia and His Grace, Bishop Valerian, in the US agreed with Sister Ileana. In the summer of 1964, Mother Eudoxia, Sister Ileana, and Mother Mary traveled to the US together to scout possible locations for a monastery.

They found two that looked suitable, and Sister Ileana was able, out of her own funds along with money that Bishop Valerian had raised, to buy both properties. One was in Nevada, where she had lived while awaiting her divorce from Dr. Issarescu just before she took her first vows as a monastic, and the other was in western Pennsylvania.

Sister Ileana felt strongly that a pan-Orthodox, English-language monastery was needed, one that would appeal to all North American Orthodox, regardless of their roots. In order to accomplish that aim, she had to interest the hierarchs of other jurisdictions in the project. Normally, a simple nun wouldn't get the time of day from anyone outside her own monastery. But because she was still revered and respected as Princess Ileana, and because hierarchs are human too—as eager as the rest of us to meet a real princess—she was able to gain appointments with them. Once in their presence, Sister Ileana displayed the expertise and experience that Princess Ileana had accumulated over a lifetime of dealing with authority. This, as well as her royal status and her obvious sincerity and conviction, impressed the bishops. She received the "blessings, prayers and best wishes" of Metropolitan Irenei of what would become the Orthodox Church in America, Archbishop Iakovos of the Greek Archdiocese, and Metropolitan Philip of the Antiochian Archdiocese.

Metropolitan Ireney accepted the potential monastery into his jurisdiction under the spiritual guidance of Valerian, who was now an archbishop.

In late 1964 or early 1965, after the trip to America with Mother Eudoxia and Mother Mary, Mother Eudoxia decided "to my unspeakable joy" that Sister Ileana was ready for the next step in the monastic life—that of ryasaphore—which is a deeper and more serious commitment to monasticism. In addition to the habit she was already wearing, Sister Ileana was blessed to wear the *klobuk** and the *ryasa.**

The English translation of the services Mother Mary had been working on took on a new significance. It would provide the basis for the monastery's work in North America. Mother Mary stepped up her efforts and enlisted the help of Father, later Bishop, Kallistos (Timothy) Ware, in England. Their translations of the *Octoechos*, the *Lenten Triodion*, and the *Festal Menaion** for the planned monastery

Sister Ileana tonsured as a ryasaphore nun

are still used today in English-language Orthodox churches in the United States and Canada.

Discussions about the location of the monastery continued with Mother Eudoxia and Archbishop Valerian. Sister Ileana was attracted to Nevada because of the desert—a very real reminder of the rigors of the monastic life. But its very isolation counted against it. This monastery, unlike any other before it, had a twofold purpose—it had to establish the monastic tradition in a new land by educating the laity about monasticism, and it had to provide a quiet and serene place for the women called to that life.

The Pennsylvania site was located in a strongly Orthodox area, almost exactly halfway between Chicago and New York City. It was within a day's drive of several major cities, including Washington, DC, and Toronto, Canada. Not only would it be accessible to devout Orthodox who felt the need either to retreat from the world for a time or to dedicate their entire lives to God, but Sister Ileana would be in the heart of a population she felt called to educate about monasticism and the faith.

Even so, establishing the monastery was not an easy task. The land was there, but there were no buildings, no services, not even, at first, a road. Most important, there were no other monastics.

Section VI

The Way to Peace

TIMELINE 1967–1991

YEAR	COUNTRY	EVENT
1967	France/USA	Ileana takes final vows as monastic, becomes Mother Alexandra; returns to USA to build and open Orthodox Monastery of the Transfiguration; Sister Despina joins the monastery
1968	USA	Monastery dedicated and altar consecrated
	Austria	Gregor (Niki's son) and Margareta (Herzi's daughter) born
	Canada	Pierre Elliot Trudeau becomes prime minister; separatist movement turns violent
	USA	Richard Nixon elected president; Martin Luther King and Robert Kennedy assassinated
1969	USA	Mother Alexandra formally installed as abbess of Orthodox Monastery of the Transfiguration
	Austria	Andrea (Herzi's daughter) born
1971	Austria	Elisabeth (Herzi's daughter) born
1972		Sandi divorced
	USA	Watergate scandal; last troops withdrawn from Vietnam
1973		Sandi remarries
	USA	End of US involvement in Vietnam War; Watergate scandal
	Greece	Monarchy abolished
1976	Austria	Baillou (Sandi's son) stillborn
	Romania	Nadia Comaneci earns gold, silver, and bronze medals at Olympics
	USA	Nation's bicentennial; James Carter elected president
1978	USA	Mother Benedicta arrives at Transfiguration Monastery to help, monastery begins to grow in numbers; Nicholas (Ileana's brother) dies at age 75
	USA	Middle East peace talks begin at Camp David
1979	USA	Mother Alexandra breaks hip, requires full replacement; Ileana (Stefan's daughter) married
	Britain	Margaret Thatcher re-elected

YEAR	COUNTRY	EVENT
1979	Canada	Joe Clark elected prime minister
	USA	Establishes full diplomatic relations with China
1981	USA	Mother Alexandra retires as abbess; Mother Benedicta appointed acting superior. Mother Alexandra writes *The Holy Angels*; continues spiritual direction, traveling and speaking about Orthodox monasticism
	Britain	Princess Alice, last surviving grandchild of Queen Victoria, dies
1982	USA	Mother Alexandra forced to wear steel-and-leather back brace to support back and to accept a cell attendant
	Canada	Canada's constitution patriated; Canada gains full political independence from the UK
1984	USA	Alexandra Snyder (Ileana's child, Stefan's grandchild, Mother Alexandra's first great-grandchild) born
	Canada	Pierre Trudeau retires, replaced by John Turner
	USA	Eastern bloc boycotts Olympic Games in Los Angeles
1986	USA	Orthodox Monastery of the Transfiguration given blessing to expand to accommodate larger number of nuns; Mother Benedicta retires, Mother Christophora appointed interim abbess
	USA	Space shuttle Challenger explodes just after launch
1987	USA	Mother Alexandra moves to St. Brigid's House to accommodate reduced mobility; Mother Christophora elected abbess
	Lebanon	British Terry Waite captured in Beirut while negotiating hostage release
1989	USA	Mother Alexandra turns 80 years old
	Romania	Week-long series of revolts overthrows Nicolae Ceausescu's communist government
	Britain	Cause of explosion of Pan Am 103 found to be a bomb
	Canada–USA	Free trade agreement takes effect
1990	Romania	Mother Alexandra returns to Romania to visit
1991	USA	Ground-breaking for expansion of monastery; Mother Alexandra breaks hip, suffers massive heart attack; reposes January 21

CHAPTER TWENTY-FOUR

The Monastic Life

The Spirit of the Lord is upon Me, because of which He anointed Me.
(Isaiah 61:1)

To many, monasticism appears to be a selfish withdrawal from the world—ignoring the plight of God's creation to concentrate solely on one's own salvation. Sister Ileana was a puzzle to many—how could she withdraw from life when she was always traveling around? Wasn't she just an overprivileged princess playing at being a nun? In truth, Sister Ileana was doing exactly what monastics do: she was submitting to the will of God.

Ileana was as much a nun while she was visiting her children and grandchildren or talking to church members about Orthodox Christianity as she was when she stood before the iconostasis* in prayer with her sisters. "A nun is a nun always," a group of monastics wrote, not because of the habit they wear or their absence from the world, but because of an inner transformation.

In order to understand how Ileana could be a monastic and still move in the world, it helps to understand, as far as laypeople can, what monasticism and a monastery are.

The monastic call has been described as "a love story" and the "expression of the soul's innermost self." A person yearns to have a closer experience of God, to be constantly in His presence. Some people take part-time jobs to leave more time for prayer. Their vacations are spent in churches and at monasteries instead of on beaches or at tourist attractions. Everything becomes secondary to the desire to "seek him whom my soul loves" (Song of Solomon 3:2).

When a person decides she must live a monastic life, she is not withdrawing from the world, monastics insist. The monastery is a haven for those who need the concentration and serenity of God's presence, and not all of those are monastics.

As long as there have been monasteries, there has been room in them for the traveler or the world-weary. In the Eastern Christian understanding, the guesthouse is a place for laypeople to bask in the peace of the monastery, to think and pray over the problems of their lives. They do not leave their problems outside the door, and it is a monastic duty to listen to and offer prayer for visitors and their difficulties.

Just as parishes offer prayers for the families of their members and for world crises, so does the monastery pray for the world. The list of intercessions in a monastic liturgy often includes more lay names than monastic names.

But monasteries cannot offer that peace and the continuing sense of God's presence if the monastics themselves do not have it, or if the monastery is in the midst of noise and confusion, whether material or spiritual.

In teaching and lecturing, Sister Ileana was laying the foundation in North America for this understanding of the monastic life. She taught her people that, just as their Romanian ancestors had needed and loved the monks and nuns who prayed constantly for God's mercy for all, so too could modern North Americans benefit from monastic peace and serenity. Sister Ileana believed "that there is a crying need for Orthodox monastic institutions in this country, especially for the English speaking faithful. I believe that God has called me to this specific work."

There are no set times or exams to take to become a fully professed monastic in the Orthodox Church. It is individual to each soul, and the monastic's superior must, through observation, prayer, and humble discernment, determine when the monk or nun has proven his or her commitment to the full task of learning to submit to God's will.

Sister Ileana's dedication had grown in the six years she had lived in

Bussy-en-Othe, and in 1967, Mother Eudoxia determined that she was ready for her tonsuring.

Imagine This

It is Lazarus Saturday—the last day of Lent, the beginning of Holy Week. A fitting day to die to the old self and be reborn as a new creature in God, a wonderful day for the prodigal to return to her Father's arms. The sun is shining and the flowers are beginning to bloom in the garden of the monastery at Bussy.

Mother Eudoxia leads Sister Ileana into the church and around the icons, to venerate every one of them, until she stands at the iconostasis before the icon of Jesus. Assisted by other nuns, Mother removes Sister Ileana's clothing until she stands in her simple white chemise. After prayers, Mother Eudoxia leads her to the narthex,* where, covered in the abbess's *mantia*,* Sister Ileana re-enters the church on her knees, prostrating* at the entrance and in the middle of the church.

"Make haste to open Your fatherly arms to me, who have wasted my life like a prodigal son," the choir sings. "Despise not a heart grown poor, O Savior, who have before Your eyes the boundless riches of Your mercies."

Sister Ileana makes one more prostration and lies on the floor until the priest-monk helps her to her feet. He questions her intentions, making sure that she is committing herself to this life of her own free will.

"Will you live in poverty for the rest of your life?"

Her eyes dimming with tears of joy, she replies, "Yes, God helping me."

"Will you live in chastity for the rest of your life?"

"Yes, God helping me."

"Will you be obedient to your superiors and to God?"

"Yes, God helping me."

After instructing her on the life she is entering, Father indicates the scissors lying on the Gospel book. She picks them up and gives them to him. He places them back on the Gospel book. Twice more she hands them to him and he replaces them, to indicate, again, that this is done of her own will.

He tonsures* her as a baby is tonsured at baptism, snipping bits of her hair, which has grown long and grey during the six years of the novitiate. This is a sign that she has renounced the world and her self-will.

As the priest cuts her hair, she gasps and closes her eyes. She feels squeezed, pushed down, and tightened, the way she felt when, as a tiny child, she rode Carol's trains through the tunnels. But this tunnel is a ring of fire, with flames leaping all around her, burning but not hurting, consuming but not destroying.

"Be known from now on as Mother Alexandra," he says.

Mother Eudoxia and the others move forward and dress the new Mother Alexandra. First her *paramandis*—a square of cloth embroidered with a cross and symbols of the crucifixion that is worn like a tiny backpack, to remind her of her promise of poverty and that Jesus offers an easy yoke and a light burden.

Next they slip the black dress on her. It signifies spiritual gladness and joy in Christ, and the black leather belt that is fastened at her waist symbolizes the mastering of the passions. Her ryasa, the robe she'd been given upon becoming a ryasaphore, and her mantia, the long pleated cape of a professed monastic, represent the vestments of salvation. After these, she dons her veil and *skufia*.* She's given a prayer rope—her spiritual sword, and a reminder to always keep Jesus in her mind and heart. Finally, she is given a candle and a cross, and each of the nuns welcomes her, asking, "What is your name?"

"My name is Mother Alexandra, a sinner," she replies.

"Save yourself, and pray for us," they respond.

PHOTOS TAKEN ON THE DAY OF ILEANA'S, now Mother Alexandra's, tonsuring show a serene and joyful woman. There is a lightness and a glow to her that is rivaled only by the photos taken on her and Anton's wedding day. She seems almost to hover above the ground in the hills behind Bussy, and the light of the day is a fitting match for the glow of her joy.

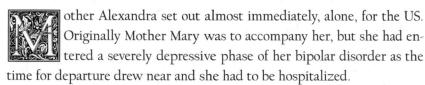

CHAPTER TWENTY-FIVE

New Life, New Home

Then He who sat on the throne said, "Behold, I make all things new."
(Revelation 21:5)

Mother Alexandra set out almost immediately, alone, for the US. Originally Mother Mary was to accompany her, but she had entered a severely depressive phase of her bipolar disorder as the time for departure drew near and she had to be hospitalized.

Mother Alexandra stayed with Stefan and his family in Farmington, Michigan, overjoyed to be with them and so close to Jackson, Michigan, where Archbishop Valerian lived.

On an overcast August day, Mother Alexandra, the building committee, and Archbishop Valerian dedicated the site of the future monastery, planting a cross where the chapel would stand, and praying for the Orthodox Monastery of the Transfiguration and for God's will to be done.

The name had been selected because, as Mother Alexandra wrote, "When the question arose as to what . . . saint or holy feast its church should be dedicated—'Transfiguration' was the immediate choice." The name reflected the monastery's mission: to create a place where "the peace that passes all understanding" could be nurtured by transforming both those who lived there and those who visited.

A board of directors was established, and almost as soon as the ink had dried on the signatures, the problems began.

The monastery grounds were not adjacent to the road, and access was through the parking lot of the Methodist church at the foot of the hill. This made access to the grounds difficult, so funds were raised to buy two lots that faced the road.

Mother Alexandra's presence was required almost constantly at the building site, and it was a long drive from her son's house in Michigan to Ellwood City, Pennsylvania. A trailer on the property, she thought, would be ideal—but there were no utilities. Instead, she found a trailer in nearby Toronto, Ohio. She set up housekeeping immediately. "Probably," she wrote, "we are the only monastery to have started out in a trailer camp!"

The monastery was to be constructed of prefabricated buildings. A large A-frame house would form the central chapel with other houses connected to it. But construction couldn't start until the road was built. That took until the end of April, and Mother Alexandra wasn't going to wait any more. She made arrangements for the trailer to be moved to the monastery grounds on the first day of May, but had forgotten to alert the authorities. Consequently, the trailer arrived in Ellwood City with a police escort, complete with flashing lights and sirens—it was almost as good as a parade!

"My first awakening on the grounds of the Monastery of the Transfiguration was heavenly," Mother Alexandra wrote. "The sun shone, the fruit trees were in blossom, the birds sang and in my heart I praised God for His great goodness. The fact that the trailer was not attached to the utilities and, not being braced yet, rocked up and down like a see-saw mattered not at all. Just to be on the property was an achievement; I could now follow the daily progress of the construction."

Mother Alexandra in front of original trailer

In Fort Wayne, Indiana, Mother Alexandra met a young convert named Despina, who had been at a convent on Patmos in Greece. She moved in with Mother Alexandra the following month.

Construction went slowly at first—twenty-one days of rain didn't help, and neither did the common habit of the construction trade—postponing the completion of little jobs if a bigger, more lucrative job comes along. "As the workmen have the upper hand, one must try and be patient, friendly (but firm) and go on nagging at them in a friendly manner—not always easy when one is boiling within," Mother Alexandra wrote to Matushka Eudoxia. It was here that Sister Despina shone. While Mother Alexandra was away on a speaking engagement, Sister Despina walked over the rise to see the progress of the work. Finding it slow to nonexistent, she lost her temper and hauled the contractor over the coals. Mother Alexandra, in her next letter to Matushka Eudoxia, was amazedly grateful and said that since it had happened, the work had sprinted forward. Mother Alexandra was so confident that she set the consecration date for September 28.

Grass sod was laid, a complete surprise to Mother Alexandra, who wrote to Matushka that she "didn't know one could buy grass by the yard!"

The date for the consecration grew closer, and the work progressed, but not quickly enough. When Matushka Eudoxia and Mother Theodosia arrived, Mother Alexander and Sister Despina were still living in the trailer, although guest rooms in the building were finished enough to accommodate the two senior nuns. The kitchen wasn't ready, so cooking was done in the trailer.

Imagine This

The day is hot for late September, but a cool breeze blows over the hill, ruffling Mother Alexandra's veil. She smoothes it down and gazes about her as the final words of the dismissal ring over the crowd. People move to venerate the cross as she and Mother Eudoxia find chairs and sit, enjoying the sun, the breeze, and the day.

"It's been a good day," says Mother Eudoxia. "Glory to God. The buildings are up, the altar consecrated, the first liturgy held. You are on your way, with God's grace and help."

Mother Alexandra nods, more than content. A glow of joy covers her, filling every corner of her being as she looks around at the colorful crowds milling about the monastery's lawn and grounds.

As she turns to speak to Mother Eudoxia, a middle-aged woman rushes up to her.

"Mother, people want to eat, now that liturgy is over, but the food's not been blessed."

Mother points to a pair of priests talking not too far away. "Ask Father John to bless the food now, and people can begin eating. Is there more coffee being made?"

The woman nods. "And tea as well."

"Good. Make sure that one of the tables is set aside for the hierarchs so they have enough when they've finished changing. Will there be enough food for everyone?"

The woman nods. "Plenty of food, you needn't worry about that. You may not have to cook for a week after this!"

"Good. But make sure you save some for the priests and bishops."

"And for you, Mother. I'll bring you both a plate, if you like." Mother Alexandra nods and smiles her thanks as the woman bustles away, gathering Father John as she goes.

Procession at the consecration of the chapel at the Monastery of the Transfiguration

A group of clergy stroll by, heading for the tent set up near the trailer where they had vested.

"What do you suppose they have for lunch?" asks a priest. "I'm hungry. Where is the food, anyway?"

A deacon points toward the trestle tables set up on the driveway. "I think that might be it," he says. "Where all the people are crowded round."

A priest cranes his neck to see where the deacon is pointing. "Well, we'd better hurry, if there's going to be any left for us!"

The pace quickens as someone asks, "How many were here, anyway?"

"About a thousand, I'd guess," says one priest. "Too bad the chapel was so small, but it would have been impossible to fit so many in for the consecration of the altar. Good thinking, to have the liturgy out here in the open air."

"A very good idea, Vladyka," says another priest to one of the bishops.

"It was," the bishop replies. "We did a good job organizing this, and it has come off well. So many people, it was a good thing we had prepared for it and had enough chalices on hand."

Mother Eudoxia leans toward Mother Alexandra. "Well! You'd think they'd done it all by themselves," she whispers.

Mother Alexandra smiles and nods, but before she can answer, another priest joins the group around the bishop. "It did go well, but this place is built for seven or eight! How many nuns does she have?"

"There's just the two of them right now," answers another priest.

"Well, we'll see what will happen. She has her monastery, but it'll be a job to fill it."

As they move away, Mother Alexandra smiles even more. The altar is consecrated, the building is almost finished, and that it went as well as it did today is God's doing, not hers, and not the clergy's doing, either. God will fill the cloisters in His own time. She is simply grateful and content that so much has already been accomplished.

The monastery as Mother Alexandra built it

THE TEST CAME after the clergy had packed their vestments, the crowds had dispersed, and the dishes were done. Mother Eudoxia and Mother Theodosia went home, and as Mother Alexandra wrote her spiritual mother, she and Sister Despina "did their best to keep the monastic rule." They said Matins, the Hours, Vespers, and Compline, using Mother Mary's translations. With her lack of musical talent, Mother Alexandra read whatever parts of the service could be read, while Sister Despina sang the responses, the troparia and kontakia.*

They attended Sunday liturgy at St. Elias Romanian Orthodox Church in Ellwood City, as well as other area churches, to help spread the word about monasticism. On more than one occasion, parishioners would take Mother Alexandra aside and whisper, "Oh, Sister, we don't have nuns in the Orthodox Church. The Catholic Church is down the street."

The priest at St. Elias, Fr. Anchidim Useriu, and other area clergy came up to the monastery to serve weekday liturgy. Sister Despina sang the responses, and Mother served in the altar as ecclesiarch.*

Mother Alexandra was formally installed as abbess on March 25, 1969.

In the early 1970s, Sister Catherine joined the monastery. She stayed for years, working with Mother Alexandra and Sister Despina. Other women were now coming to test their intent. They stayed for varying lengths of time, but none committed—the visits varied from a few days to several months, and as Mother Alexandra noted, "They comes and they goes, but mostly they goes."

She was still traveling, giving talks on Orthodox monasticism all over the US, Eastern Canada, and Europe. She continued to record for Radio Free Europe.

But the years, the work both in and outside the monastery, and her health were beginning to take their toll. In 1975, she was 66. Her back kept her in constant pain. She was in and out of the hospital for that and other problems. Her tear ducts dried up, although she liked to say that she'd cried all the tears that were in her years before. To give her more solitude and rest, the monastery built a small house a little way up from the cloister, toward the forest at the back of the property. Called St. Anne's House, it was modeled after the cottage her sister Lisabeta had designed and her father had built for her at Scroviste years before. The front window overlooked the wide, green meadow and the foothills of the Allegheny Mountains, which so reminded her of home—although, as she pointed out, in Romania the meadow in front of St. Anne's would be planted with flowers, all one color from hill to hill! She could sit on a deck around the house in her rare free moments and enjoy the deer, who lived in the woods only twenty feet from her door.

As far as she could, Mother Alexandra kept active and busy. Her work as a spiritual director was growing and she advised many people, not the least of whom were her family. In a letter to her brother, Nicolas, written in 1976, she advised him to forgive his family for the hurts of years ago: "Forgiveness . . . always makes sense, especially . . . with such few remaining members. Furthermore, we are united by a past that has not always been dark; on the contrary, we are tied together by many happy, bright and cheerful memories."

She met Father Roman Braga, a refugee from the Romanian concentration camps, at the Vatra in Michigan. His sister, Mother Benedicta, managed to obtain permission from Romania to come to the US for a visit. She stayed at Transfiguration Monastery and offered to move to the US to help Mother Alexandra.

Mother Benedicta was in many ways a blessing for both the monastery and Mother Alexandra. Although she had spent six years in the monastery in France, Mother Alexandra did not have the experience of a fully professed monastic, living a long and uninterrupted life in the monastic routine. Mother Benedicta, with fifty years of monasticism behind her, had the wealth of tradition built into her bones.

It took time, but in September 1978 the monastery boasted more nuns than it had ever had before: there were four women to sing the services, look after the monastery's dogs, speak at churches in the area, and learn to submit their lives to God's will. It was obvious that in spite of her elementary grasp of English, the routine and tradition Mother Benedicta brought with her was going to provide a minor revolution for the monastery.

CHAPTER TWENTY-SIX

Twilight, Daybreak

My soul magnifies the Lord,
And my spirit has rejoiced in God my Savior.
(Luke 1:46, 47)

n the instruction of Archbishop Valerian, Mother Benedicta had taken over immediately as abbess-in-fact—relegating Mother Alexandra to the sidelines in the day-to-day running of the monastery and supervision of the nuns.

While this gave Mother Alexandra the time and peace she needed, it couldn't have been easy for her. That she submitted to Mother Benedicta was an amazing act of humility. Through enormous effort Mother Alexandra had built a base of support, raised the funds to purchase the land and construct the buildings. From 1968 to 1978 she, Sister Despina, and Sister Catherine had occupied cells in a building meant for seven. The echoing silences must at times have seemed reproachful. In spite of her protestations that she always trusted in God's will, Mother Alexandra must have wondered if she had understood God correctly. To be moved to the sidelines after almost fifteen years of effort and struggle could have led to bitterness and cynicism, yet she accepted the change with no word of complaint.

In many ways, it must have been a relief to Mother Alexandra. Running any organization is hard work. There are bills to pay, income to generate, routines to establish and adhere to, and interpersonal problems to deal with. She had done all that and more in the days of the Bran hospital, but Mother Alexandra was now in her seventies. She no longer had the energy or the stamina of her prime.

She also was forced to admit that her failing health would simply not allow her to do it all any longer—toward the end of 1979 she broke her hip, necessitating a full hip replacement.

Her official retirement in 1981, at the age of 72, meant that she no longer ran the monastery, and she seemed content to have it so. Certainly it was in capable hands.

During the 1980s, the nuns at the monastery, under Mother Benedicta's care, continued Mother Alexandra's work of speaking at retreats and introducing more of the faithful to monasticism. In addition, the monastery's records reflect that the nuns were receiving visitors from other monasteries in North America. Mother Alexandra's work was bearing fruit.

Transfiguration Monastery had grown so much that by 1986, they received a blessing to expand—the original building, designed to house eight nuns, was bursting at the seams with eleven.

Also that year, in spite of being over 70, Mother Benedicta retired from Holy Transfiguration and went on to found a new, Romanian-language monastery, Holy Dormition, in Rives Junction, Michigan. She was succeeded as abbess by Mother Christophora, an American-born cradle Orthodox, in August of 1987.

Mother Alexandra's health continued to decline. In 1982, doctors insisted she wear a heavy steel-and-leather back brace, and she was forced to accept the presence of a cell attendant* or "novice" (as the attendants called themselves) to assist in her day-to-day needs. In 1987, the same year Mother Christophora became abbess, Mother Alexandra moved into a new home. The stairs at St. Anne's were too much for her, so a double-wide trailer named St. Bridget's was installed "across the street" from her old place. Unlike St. Anne's it was only a couple of steps up from the ground, and the interior was all one level.

In spite of her ill health, she kept up with her far-flung family. Ileana, Stefan's eldest daughter, married in 1979, and presented Mother Alexandra with her first great-grandchild in October of 1984. Stefan himself retired that year, and he and Mother Alexandra were in constant touch. Herzi and

Magi were busy raising their own families, while Niki and his family were based in Antigua in the West Indies. Sandi, who had divorced in 1972, re-married and worked as a nurse in Austria and as an assistant at Lourdes. Mother Alexandra's ongoing correspondence with her nephew, the exiled King Mihai, never flagged. They exchanged letters and Christmas cards, and she visited him in Switzerland.

Mother Alexandra had the gift of spiritual direction, and over the years had a number of people who came to depend on her for guidance. She kept contact with her spiritual children, writing, calling, and receiving them when they visited the monastery.

Her fame grew with the years. People did not forget the princess-turned-nun. Journalists, writers, and reporters sought her out for interviews and research. She turned few of them down, maintaining that it was her duty to help wherever and however she could.

The monastery hosted a birthday celebration for Mother Alexandra in early 1989. It was her eightieth birthday, and her family—children, grand-children, and great-grandchildren—gathered with her monastic family to celebrate her life.

Mother Alexandra on her eightieth birthday with her children and grandchildren

It was later that year that God truly showed Mother Alexandra how merciful He is. On December 17, 1989, the dictator of Romania, Ceausescu, was overthrown, and for a time it looked as if democracy would triumph. Ileana was overjoyed: her people, at long last, were free from oppression and terror, something she hadn't expected to happen in her lifetime. She could finally speak on the record about the suffering of the Romanians. For a time, the monastery "crawled with reporters and photographers." More joy was to come—she obtained permission, not only from King Mihai, but also from the Romanian government, to travel to her homeland. She felt especially drawn to the plight of the thousands of orphans, many of them with AIDS.

A few days before her departure in September of 1990, Mother Alexandra went to St. Elizabeth's Hospital. The pain she lived in was virtually uncontrollable, and she received injections of painkiller directly into her spine to try to control the worst of it. She still considered her physical problems a bore, though, and once commented that "the only part of me that doesn't hurt is my artificial hip."

As Mother Alexandra wished, her cell attendant left her in the waiting room to run errands. When she returned, she found Mother Alexandra flat out on the floor. Mother Alexandra was treated for cardiac failure and reluctantly released, but was advised to cancel her trip. "Will you?" asked the cell attendant.

Mother Alexandra shook her head. She did agree to tell Sandi, her daughter, whom she visited before entering Romania. Sandi quickly changed her plans so that she could accompany her mother.

ເວລາ ເວລາ ເວລາ Imagine This ເວລາ ເວລາ ເວລາ

Mother Alexandra stands in the little chapel at Bran, knees trembling, mouth aquiver. Tears would run down her cheeks but that she'd long ago lost her tear ducts. She's cried herself out, she tells people.

Until this moment, the reality of the trip has not penetrated. Her landing in Bucharest, stepping off the plane onto land she thought she'd never see or touch again; the memorial for her parents at their tombs in Curtea de Arges, seeing so many old friends, so many more than she thought would have survived! It's felt like a waking dream. Even the greetings of the people—two thousand just when she arrived here at Bran! And seeing the village woman who'd pressed the basket of fruit into her hands as they left the train station in Brasov in 1948: a true joy to give her back her basket, filled again with fruit. But the feelings are distant, as if she were dreaming it, or reliving a long-ago memory.

Even as she thinks back over the past days, standing in the tiny chapel, it still seems unreal, as though a glass plate stands between her and what is happening. Even her own emotions seem distant. Until now. Until she stands next to the tomb of the great love of her heart.

The glass unreality shatters and Mother Alexandra sinks to her knees, shoulders shaking with sobs. She touches the plaque her mother had inscribed on Mircea's tomb, traces the letters with her fingertips:

> In this sanctuary of Cotroceni, beside those who in former days were rulers of this land, lies the youngest son of King Ferdinand and Queen Marie, born December 21, 1912,‡
>
> MIRCEA
>
> died October 20, 1916, in the time of war, while the soldiers of Romania were sacrificing their lives for the dream of centuries.
>
> Two years he remained sole guardian of the home of his parents, over which the country's flag had ceased to float. Mourn for him, for he shared with us the days of suffering, but the days of rejoicing he did not live to see.

Mourn for him. How glad she was so many times in the last years that he wasn't there to mourn what had happened, and now she wishes he could be here to help her realize the reality of the freedom her people have found once again.

How good God is, she thinks. Everything she's ever wanted in life has come to be, and God has stood by her through all the pain, the exile, the heartache. Now, he has even given her back her homeland.

‡ *At the time of Mircea's death, Romania still adhered to the Julian calendar, which lags behind the Gregorian calendar (that in common use in the West) by thirteen days. By Western reckoning, Mircea was born January 2, 1913.*

And yet, even as she wishes Mircea were present, as she continues to cry for deep joy, she knows that something of both her mother, whose heart still rests in the living rock of the mountain across the way, and of her youngest brother remains. They have always been, both for her and for her people, a symbol of the love and faith that no earthly power can destroy.

STEFAN SPOKE TO HER ON HER RETURN. True to form, she was organizing aid for the hundred thousand AIDS-afflicted orphans. When he protested there were too many, she responded as she always had: "It's better to help one child than to say what we cannot do about a thousand!"

Mother Alexandra spent a quiet Christmas—overjoyed by her country's freedom and the blessing of having returned home, content in the knowledge that not only was the monastery growing in community, they were continuing the work she had begun. More and more people were coming to the monastery to learn firsthand about the peace and serenity that dedication to God can bring.

CHAPTER TWENTY-SEVEN

Memory Eternal

Give rest, O Lord, to the soul of your servant departed this life.
(Troparion for the departed)

❧❧❧ Imagine This ❧❧❧

It is Friday, January 4, 1991, the eve of Mother Alexandra's eighty-second birthday. Her cell attendant leaves for Vespers as usual. This evening, Mother isn't going up to the chapel. She is tired and in pain, and the walk over the snow-covered drive is too risky with her uncertain steps. The novice and Mother Alexandra will prepare dinner when she returns. Mother Alexandra enjoys playing "Julia Child" with their meals, adding seasoning and spices while the novice chops and stirs. In the meantime, she and Tom, the tiger-striped Persian cat, remain behind in St. Bridget's house.

Afterward, the attendant walks through the darkened evening, breathing in the crisp, cold air, feet crunching over the snow-covered ground. She enters the back hall.

"Didn't Mother put the news on, Tom?" she asks as the cat comes to greet her, noting the darkened and silent house.

"Mother, I think I've broken my hip," calls the voice from the living room.

The cell attendant hurries, turning on lights. Mother Alexandra lies on the floor, gazing fixedly at the Mother of God icon.

A call to the monastery, and controlled pandemonium ensues. Mother Alexandra directs traffic from the floor and is transported by ambulance to St. Elizabeth's Hospital in Youngstown, Ohio, an hour's drive to the west.

The night is spent in the emergency room, where blood is drawn, tests are conducted. Mother Alexandra is X-rayed, her heart monitored, and she and her attendant wait for the doctor's prognosis. She scribbles a note to her sisters: "I am ok. Don't worry, operation after 11 AM, love all, MA."

Later that day, Mother Alexandra suffers a mild heart attack. She's moved to the cardiac unit, where another massive attack comes, incapacitating a full third of her heart muscle and partially collapsing her lung.

Stefan arrives, and then Magi and Herzi. Sandi stays in Europe to be the communication link to the European branches of the family.

Until Mother Alexandra recovers from the attack and its effects, surgery is unthinkable. She needs mechanical assistance to begin healing, so she consents to the IV, the intubations, wires and monitors banked behind her bed.

It causes no end of anxiety to the nurses as her lips move constantly during and after the procedure—they think she is trying to speak to them around the tube invading her throat, but her novice explains. "Although she could not make a sound now . . . the rhythm was easy to lip-read: 'Jesus Christ, Son of God, have mercy on me!' . . . In the midst of the clanging, beeping, flashing machinery . . . communication with the Lord of Hosts!"

It's clear to the cell attendant and to Stefan, Magi, and Herzi that this is torture to Mother Alexandra—she is in more pain than she's ever known, she hates the sound of the mechanical devices behind her, and every breath is agony. Her cell attendant writes that in voluntarily accepting the mechanized assistance, "Mother Alexandra experienced the torture of her own Romanians in prison camps where inhuman torture to break their will was inflicted upon them . . . no longer was her suffering mere empathy and vicarious, but real and experiential."

Her monastic family visits whenever they can, along with Father Joseph, her priest. They sing molebens* and say prayers with her and for her recovery. "The singing and chanting seemed to give lift to her heart," her cell attendant wrote, "perhaps reinforcing the strength of its beat. . . . Hymns and tropars slipped into her heart's chambers to make an acrostic with the Jesus Prayer which was already there. The 'heart' is not only the physical organ of four ventricles, but the whole person, the will, the love, the intellect. . . . Prayers, Psalms, hymns are the background music in the monastic's life," and it is these that help sustain Mother Alexandra for the last weeks of her life.

Over the next few days there is a slight improvement. The cardiologist says there is one more, risky surgical procedure he can try. "After a serious conference between the doctors, the family and the nuns, we decide that it is worth taking the risk," writes Stefan.

The operation doesn't help. In order to make her more comfortable, the families decide to remove the respirator and move her from cardiac ICU to a private room. Quiet and peace are the last gifts her loved ones can offer.

The removal of some of the equipment seems to help. Stefan gets her to sip some water and eat some applesauce.

Mother Alexandra's skin is unbearably tender, and the elastic cord holding her oxygen mask in place feels like rough sandpaper rasping her cheeks. The pressure of the mask cuts like a knife. In an act of pure devotion, Herzi, Magi, Stefan, and the novice take turns by the hour holding the oxygen mask over Mother Alexandra's nose and mouth to ease the pain.

Sleep deprivation from the machines and the heart damage brings demonic hallucinations and nightmares when Mother Alexandra manages to drift off. Between the nuns praying, and Stefan and Magi improvising, they defeat the enemy and help Mother Alexandra sleep restfully.

Mother Christophora comes as often as she can with news of the monastery, and on the sixteenth is able to tell Mother Alexandra that the foundations for the expansion have been poured. She smiles her joy at the continuing realization of God's work and her dream.

She seems to improve but, as Stefan writes, "Her heart is still damaged, she has had no significant food by mouth for almost three weeks, her leg is still broken and the doctors tell me there is a high chance of pneumonia developing." The doctors are honest—pain alleviation is the best they can do.

On Sunday, January 20, Mother Alexandra receives Holy Communion and the Sacrament of Holy Unction. The prayers at the time of the parting of the soul are read over her.

Monday the twenty-first dawns cold and overcast but bright. It is snowing, and Mother Alexandra comments to her cell attendant that it is "as white as the Transfiguration."

Bishop Nathaniel, an old and dear friend, comes by. He gives her his blessing. They have been close and loving friends throughout his ministry. He has supported and sustained the monastery and her vision since before the property was selected.

Stefan and his mother talk quietly, the cell attendant nearby. Mother Alexandra's eyelids sink; she takes a breath, and slowly, another.

"God is light, God is with us," says the attendant. One last breath, and Mother Alexandra is with God, with the angels whom she saw so many years ago, and with the saints who sustained and supported her in her life's work.

"My last prayer is that the Lord God let the light of His Face shine upon you and bestow upon you the joy that no man can take from you. Amen."

—Mother Alexandra, Ileana, Princess of Romania

Epilogue

rincess Ileana's royal birth was announced by a twenty-one-gun salute, and Mother Alexandra was laid to rest by the repeated singing of the Thrice Holy Hymn and the tolling of the monastery bells. The pot of Romanian soil she'd treasured all the years of her exile was buried with her. At her funeral a host of monks and nuns crowded the small chapel she built here in 1968. They represented new Orthodox monasteries springing up throughout the US—new monasteries based on Mother Alexandra's vision to live the Orthodox monastic life in America. Her vision, no longer an oddity, has borne fruit.

After reading about this princess turned nun, you may be thinking, "What a remarkable woman; what a remarkable life." As difficult as her life was, she learned, as did St. Paul, to be content in whatever state she found herself (see Philippians 4:11). And she also learned very early in her life to work—to do something, anything, to help others whenever she could and wherever she found herself.

Her faithfulness and her labor bore fruit—and among the many fruits of Mother Alexandra's life is the monastery she founded. Knowing what a spiritual wealth is found in monasticism, Mother Alexandra offered her efforts to bring this treasure to the American land. Those of us who live in the monastery, as well as the many pilgrims who visit, know how blessed is the piece of land on which it is built, ever emitting the light of Tabor to all who seek Him here.

A strong part of the legacy Mother Alexandra left us is her emphasis on developing relationships with others, Orthodox and non-Orthodox, and offering to them spiritual food as well as hospitality. Mother Alexandra laid the foundation for these relationships, using her wisdom and her training as a member of the royalty to develop them. As a result, this monastery has become known throughout the Orthodox world, hosting visiting hierarchs, clergy, monastics, and laity from all over the Americas as well as countries across the sea. She desired a haven of peace where God's presence is clear, and truly these many pilgrims attest that her desire has been fulfilled. Some stay with us for a few hours, others for a week or more. Often they tell the nuns how deeply their stay has affected them—they have found peace, the answers to questions, healing of soul, and most importantly have felt the presence of their Lord. When visitors come, or when members of our monastic community travel throughout the country speaking at retreats and church functions, there are many questions about and much interest in the life of Mother Alexandra.

The spirit of Mother Alexandra is with us here. She once told an interviewer, "I feel that the Lord is never far from me." We feel that our foundress is never far from us. The example she left us of stability, endurance,

courage, compassion, of a humility born from suffering, and of faith, a strong hope, and hard-won peace gives each one of us the strength needed to persevere. She often told the nuns that "we must do what we can," little by little finding God, ourselves, and our neighbor. She advised, "We must not fear to face the storm; rather, unflinchingly, we must look into the midst of it so as to see the saving truth." Readers can see from this biography that Mother Alexandra faced many storms in her life, and by staring into the midst of them unflinchingly, she acquired a deep compassion for human frailty and a boundless trust in the mercy of God. This was the bedrock upon which she built this monastery. Our foundress taught us to strive continually toward the reality of heaven while doing our duty in the here and now, putting the good of pilgrims and our sisterhood above our own.

Prayers for the peaceful repose of our beloved Mother Alexandra continue to be offered in our chapel, and in churches and monasteries throughout the world. We thank God for the extraordinary example she has set for us by the way she lived a life full of heartbreaks, illnesses, and trials, as well as the presence and joy of her Lord. These verses from the Wisdom of Solomon truly can be applied to Mother Alexandra:

> *For though in man's view they were punished,*
> *Their hope is full of immortality.*
> *Though chastened in a few things,*
> *Great kindness will be shown them,*
> *For God tested them and found them worthy of Himself.*
> *He tested them like gold in a furnace*
> *And accepted them as a whole burnt offering. (3:4–6)*

Her lovingly tended grave is an often-visited site. Sometimes we go for a moment of quiet, or to ask for her guidance and strength in our struggles, or to sing a hymn of thanksgiving for her labors here. On occasion, we find gifts left by grateful pilgrims—flowers, a candle, a seashell. What is perhaps her strongest legacy to us all, lay and monastic alike, is inscribed on her gravestone:

> *None of us lives to himself, and none of us dies to himself. If we live, we live to the Lord, and if we die, we die to the Lord; so then, whether we live or whether we die, we are the Lord's (Romans 14:7–8).*

> *The Sisters of the Orthodox Monastery of the Transfiguration*
> *Ellwood City, PA*

Princess Ileana's Family Tree

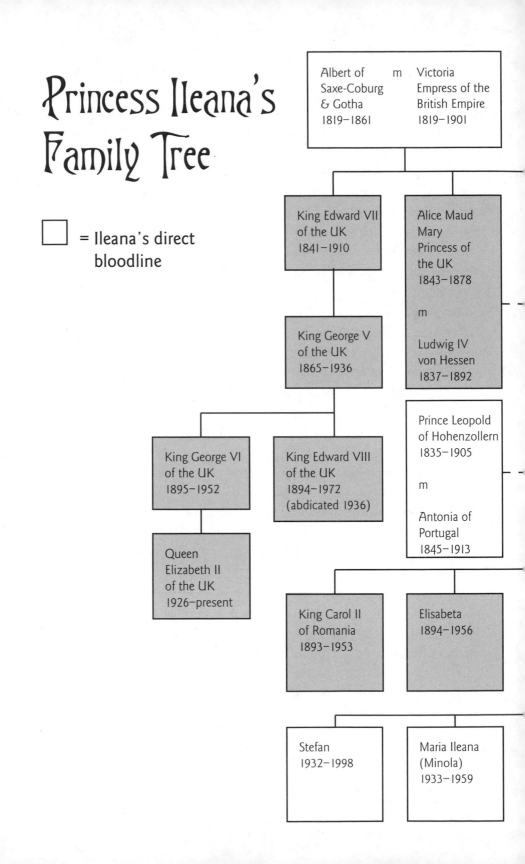

= Ileana's direct bloodline

Albert of Saxe-Coburg & Gotha 1819–1861 m Victoria Empress of the British Empire 1819–1901

King Edward VII of the UK 1841–1910

Alice Maud Mary Princess of the UK 1843–1878

m

Ludwig IV von Hessen 1837–1892

King George V of the UK 1865–1936

Prince Leopold of Hohenzollern 1835–1905

m

Antonia of Portugal 1845–1913

King George VI of the UK 1895–1952

King Edward VIII of the UK 1894–1972 (abdicated 1936)

Queen Elizabeth II of the UK 1926–present

King Carol II of Romania 1893–1953

Elisabeta 1894–1956

Stefan 1932–1998

Maria Ileana (Minola) 1933–1959

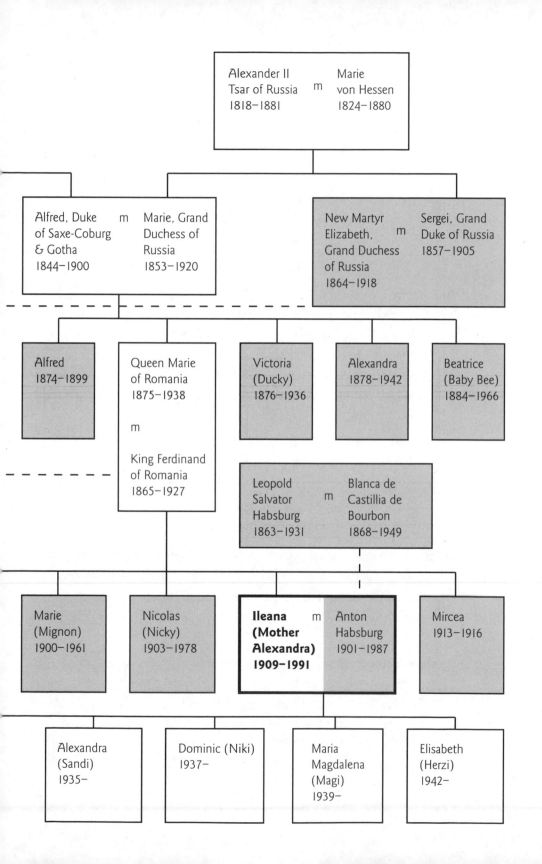

Alexander II
Tsar of Russia
1818–1881

m

Marie
von Hessen
1824–1880

Alfred, Duke
of Saxe-Coburg
& Gotha
1844–1900

m

Marie, Grand
Duchess of
Russia
1853–1920

New Martyr
Elizabeth,
Grand Duchess
of Russia
1864–1918

m

Sergei, Grand
Duke of Russia
1857–1905

Alfred
1874–1899

Queen Marie
of Romania
1875–1938

m

King Ferdinand
of Romania
1865–1927

Victoria
(Ducky)
1876–1936

Alexandra
1878–1942

Beatrice
(Baby Bee)
1884–1966

Leopold
Salvator
Habsburg
1863–1931

m

Blanca de
Castillia de
Bourbon
1868–1949

Marie
(Mignon)
1900–1961

Nicolas
(Nicky)
1903–1978

**Ileana
(Mother
Alexandra)
1909–1991**

m

Anton
Habsburg
1901–1987

Mircea
1913–1916

Alexandra
(Sandi)
1935–

Dominic (Niki)
1937–

Maria
Magdalena
(Magi)
1939–

Elisabeth
(Herzi)
1942–

Glossary

Anschluss   The March 1938 annexation of Austria by Germany. It was a political coup engineered by both the German Nazi government and the Austrian Nazi party. On the day before the plebiscite held to determine whether the two countries should unite, the Austrian National Socialist Party seized internal power and transferred political power to Germany, who sent in the Wehrmacht troops to enforce the unification.

Astrakhan   Refers to the curly wool of young lambs from Astrakhan, or to fabric with a curly loopy pile made to resemble the wool.

Beteala   Beteala are spun gold threads draped on a bride's head or over her veil. The tradition dates to pre-Roman times, when the threads may have constituted a dowry for the bride.

Billet   A billet is the place where a soldier is assigned to sleep. In situations like war, there are often no official barracks for a detachment, and so the civilian population is expected to "billet" the soldiers—provide sleeping accommodation for them, and often cooking facilities as well.

Bolshevik Revolution   An eight-month upheaval in Russia beginning with the February Revolution in 1917, which led directly to the fall of Tsar Nicholas II (Ileana's cousin) and to the creation of a provisional government that hoped to establish a democratic republic. Instead, the release of the Bolshevik leaders led to the October Revolution in 1917 and the eventual (1922) establishment of the USSR.

Brasov   Industrial city in Transylvania, pronounced "Brashov"

Bulldog Drummond   The main character in a series of detective novels written by "Sapper" (Herman Cyril McNeile), which during the 1920s and 1930s were as popular and well-known as Sherlock Holmes.

Cell attendant   A nun who lives with and aids an older nun. Usually someone with nursing training who can do basic nursing care and first aid and assess the elder's condition.

Central Powers   The alliance of Germany, Austria-Hungary, the Ottoman Empire, and Bulgaria that fought against the Allies in WWI. The name comes from the location of these countries—between the Russian Empire in the east and France and Great Britain in the west.

Cossack   Cossacks are a community of martial people living in the southern steppe regions of Eastern Europe—primarily Russia and Ukraine. They are famous for their military units and especially for their cavalry, as well as for their distinctive uniforms, which were copied by fashion designers for their clean, striking elegance and simplicity.

Cotroceni   A disused monastery on the outskirts of Bucharest, which Princess Marie took over and turned into a palace just after she and Ferdinand married. They raised their family there, and when Ferdinand became king, it became the official royal residence.

Domnitza   Romanian: Princess, Your Highness

Ecclesiarch   In the Orthodox Church, the term *ecclesiarch* can designate a person who cares for the altar and its contents, a person who arranges the services, or in a women's monastery, with a priest's blessing, an ecclesiarch may also function as an altar server or acolyte.

Gestapo   Official secret police of Nazi Germany. Their job was to investigate and combat "all tendencies dangerous to the state" in any way they wanted. As long as they were carrying out the will of the leaders, they were acting legally, and were not accountable to anyone but Hitler and his immediate circle.

Girl Reserves of YWCA   See *Junior Red Cross*.

Guiding Movement; Girl Guides   Lord Baden Powell began the Girl

Guides in England in 1909. They are known as "Girl Guides" or "Girl Scouts" now, but at first many people referred to the organization as "the Guiding Movement."

Heimatlos   Austrian term, literally meaning "homelandless" or stateless. It means a person who has lost his citizenship, or had it removed from him, and hence belongs nowhere.

Iconostasis   "Icon screen": a false wall with doors, covered with icons, that separates the altar area from the sanctuary in an Orthodox church or chapel.

Infanta   A Spanish and Portuguese term for "princess."

Isprava   Romanian for "Fortunate Adventure."

Jassy (Iasi)   Capital city of Moldavia, pronounced "Yosh" or "Yawsh"

Junior Red Cross; Girl Reserves of YWCA   The 1920s to the 1950s were a time when many social service organizations were active for adults as well as for children. The Red Cross formed a "Junior" Red Cross and the international YWCA (Young Women's Christian Association), or Women's Christian Association as it was known in Romania, also formed groups for young people. The groups Ileana belonged to did mostly social work—aiding the poor, the destitute, the disabled, and the homebound and those affected by the war and by natural disasters.

Klobuk   The hat worn by women monastics.

Klondike   A river and a geographical area in the Yukon Territories in Canada. Also refers to the Klondike Gold Rush, when gold was found in the Klondike River near Dawson City in the late 1800s.

Liturgy   The central service of the Orthodox Christian Church—roughly equivalent to the Roman Catholic Mass, or Eucharist service.

Luftwaffe   German term meaning "air force."

Mantia   A pleated cape worn by fully professed nuns.

Moleben   A supplicatory service said for a particular purpose. It can be said for a particular saint or need, such as thanks for blessings received, or for the ill or when leaving on a journey. It can also be said to commemorate a particular saint or day, or to recognize a particular time or event, such as the beginning of school or the new year.

Narthex   Enclosed passage between the door and the sanctuary of a church.

Octoechos, Lenten Triodion, Festal Menaion   Service books containing the variable texts used in Orthodox services.

Prostration   The act of kneeling and touching one's forehead to the floor, or lying full length on the floor during prayer or before an altar, an icon, or the consecrated host. It's an act of submission, humility, and adoration.

Reich   German word meaning "empire," "realm," or "nation." Its most common association is with Hitler's Germany, which was also known as the "Third Reich." As his territory expanded in the late 1930s and through the early years of the war, the Reich meant not only Germany, but all the conquered territories as well.

Romania Mare   Greater Romania. In the settlement after WWI, Romania was granted some of its traditional lands (see map on page 12), which included Bessarabia, Bukovina, the Dobrudja, and Transylvania. These territories remained part of Romania until 1940, when Hitler ceded Bessarabia to the USSR and gave most of the Dobrudja to Bulgaria, which resulted in the forced abdication of King Carol II.

Russian Revolution *(see also Bolshevik Revolution)*   The Russian Revolution was a long period of growing unrest due to a number of political, economic and social factors that erupted into violence in 1916 and 1917. The tsar of Russia and the government were overthrown and replaced by a series of governments that became a communist dictatorship known as the USSR in 1922. The USSR disintegrated in 1991.

Ryasa   The black robe that goes over the nun's habit.

Skufia   The hat a monastic wears.

Stirbey, Prince Barbu   Prince Barbu Stirbey (1873–1946) was a member of the Romanian aristocracy and was briefly prime minister of

Romania in 1927. He was a close friend and trusted advisor of King
Ferdinand and especially of Queen Marie, who relied on him for political and moral support and friendship. He knew Ileana from the time
she was born, and she called him "the Good Man," relying on him for
advice in particularly difficult situations.

Sturmabteilung   German term meaning "Storm troopers." A Nazi para-
military organization, also known as "Brownshirts" for the color of their
uniform. They were thugs and bullies and were given permission to
harass and beat those they decided were enemies of the Reich and of
Hitler.

Tonsure   The cutting of hair in a religious context. It occurs at baptism
and when an individual makes his final monastic commitment, or is
ordained subdeacon, deacon, or priest. The ceremony in which a monastic makes her final vows is called her "tonsuring."

Total war   A state of war in which the government mobilizes all available resources for the support of the combat. Women are encouraged
or conscripted into the forces, or into production to free men for combat duty. Rationing for manufacturing and industry as well as the civilian population is either implemented or tightened. Manufacturers are
required to retool in order to produce more supplies for the war effort.
Also, civilians are encouraged or required to recycle as much as possible to aid the war effort; blackout conditions take effect; civilians who
are able are required and encouraged to grow their own food to free
more for the troops; and any able-bodied citizen between the mid-
teens and old age may be conscripted into the armed forces.

Troparia and kontakia   Hymns honoring a particular saint or feast day.

Tsar (Czar)   Russian term for king or emperor.

Typhoid fever   A highly contagious disease, transmitted when infected
fecal material is absorbed into the body through contaminated water
or food. While easily curable now by vaccine and antibiotics, it was
deadly in earlier centuries. It is characterized by high fever (up to 104°F
or 40°C), profuse sweating, dehydration, and diarrhea.

Typhus   Transmitted through body lice, typhus is another contagious and deadly disease. It most commonly appears in crowded and unsanitary conditions that occur during wars and natural disasters. Symptoms include headache, high fever (up to 102°F, 38°C), cough, stupor, and sensitivity to light.

Unit, raising a   In Canada and Britain, it used to be legal for private persons to finance a military unit—hence there are regiments such as Princess Patricia's Canadian Light Infantry, or the Canadian Scottish Regiment (Princess Mary's), or the Yukon Machine Gun Company, which was raised by Joe Boyle. These individuals didn't command the men and had no military authority over them, although their ceremonial authority was acknowledged on formal occasions.

Vatra   The Vatra is a property located in Grass Lake, Michigan. It's a summer camp, a gathering place for Romanian American Orthodox to strengthen their ties and their faith, and to give their children the experience of living an Orthodox life in summer camps.

Voivod   A Slavic term for a military commander or governor of a region. It designated the aristocracy, the dukes, earls, and princes of Romania.

Wehrmacht   The unified German forces—Air Force (Luftwaffe), Navy (Kriegsmarine), and Army (Heer).

Sources

Alexandra, Mother. *The Holy Angels*. Minneapolis: Light and Life Publishing, 1987

Bolshakoff, Serguis & Pennington, M. Basil. *In Search of True Wisdom*, Alba Press, 1991

Elsberry, Terence. *Marie of Romania*. New York: St. Martin's Press, 1972

Glennon, Joseph. "Report to Free Europe Committee," unpublished 1956, Kent State Archives

Habsburg, Stefan. "My Mama, Three Recollections: Ileana, the Princess, the New World Lecturer, the Nun: Mother Alexandra." *Information Bulletin*, edited by Traian Lascu. Jackson, MI: Romanian American Heritage Center, Jan–Feb 1992

Ileana, Princess of Romania. "The Consolation of My Grief" (clipping). *Dumineca Soliea*, April 1959

———. "I Saw It Happen," radiobroadcast Trans Radio Records, approximately 1950

———. "Focus on World Affairs." Audio recording of Foreign Policy Panel telecast, March 29, 1960

———. *I live Again*. New York: Rinehart & Company, Inc., 1952

———. *Information Bulletin*, Jackson, MI: Romanian American Heritage Center, 1961 (an open letter explaining her reasons for entering the monastic life)

———. Private lecture, May 17–18, 1953, Chicago and Evanston, Illinois

———. Private letters to Julie Thompson, 1949

———. Private letters to Mother Eudoxia, 1967–1972

———. Private letters to Nicholas Hohenzollern, 1972, translated by Valeria Motet and Mira Davidson, 2007

———, Private correspondence with HM King Michael of Romania, varying years

———, Private correspondence, articles in magazines and newspapers relating to Romania, 1967–1991. Archived at Kent State

———. *Hospital of the Queen's Heart,* New York: Rinehart & Company, Inc. 1954

Ion, Narcis Dorin. *Bran Castle—Residence of Queen Marie and Princess Ileana.* Bucharest: Editura Tritonic, 2004

Mandache Diana (ed.). *Later Chapters of My Life—The Lost Memoir of Queen Marie of Romania.* Glouchestershire: Sutton Publishing, 2004

Marie, Queen of Romania. *Ordeal: The Story of My Life,* New York: Charles Scribner's Sons, 1935

———. "The Girl with the Blue Eyes," http://www.tkinter.smig.net/PrincessIleana/BlueEyes/index.htm

Nuns of the Orthodox Monastery of the Transfiguration. Various articles in *Life Transfigured,* Ellwood City: The Orthodox Monastery of the Transifguration, 1967–2005

———. *As Silver is Tried,* unpublished memoir of Mother Alexandra's life and death, 1991 or 1992

Pakula, Hannah. *The Last Romantic – A Biography of Queen Marie of Roumania.* New York: Simon and Schuster, 1984

Sauerwein, Stan. *Klondike Joe Boyle/Heroic Adventures from Gold Fields to Battlefields.* Alberta: Stephen Hutchings 2003

Privately recorded talk by Mother Theodora at the Mother Alexandra Memorial Lecture of 2006, Orthodox Monastery of the Transfiguration

"Aunts of Michael may be exiled too," *New York Times,* New York: New York Times Jan 8, 1948. http://select.nytimes.com/gst/abstract.html?res=F30914F7355C167B93C5A9178AD85F4C8485F9&scp=1&sq=Aunts+of+Michael+may+be+exiled+too&st=p

"Alexander Cancelled," *Time Magazine,* New York: March 17, 1930. www.time.com/time/magazine/article/0,9171,738826,00.html

The Peerage.com: http://thepeerage.com/p10175.htm#i101741; http://the-peerage.com/p10074.htm#i100731

http://www.fitz-patrick.ca/ttou/chapterone/one.htm; www.fitz-patrick.ca/ttou/chapterthree/eight.htm—unpublished memoir relating to Count Alexander "Lexel" von Hochberg and his family

http://stnina.org/journal/art/3.4.6—An interview with Mother Christophora

http://www.thecanadianencyclopedia.com/index.cfm?PgNm=TCE&Params=A1ARTA0000945—Joseph Whiteside Boyle

Royal Genealogies, Part 9: http://ftp.cac.psu.edu/~saw/royal/r09.html#I309

Sources for Quotations:

Quotations from *I Live Again* found on pages: 17, 18, 25, 27, 77, 78, 88, 93, 97, 108, 132, 140, 143–46

Quotations from Queen Marie's autobiographies found on pages: 14, 17, 21, 22

Quotations from *The Holy Angels* found on pages: 18, 26, 62, 142

Quotations from *Marie of Romania* found on pages: 19, 22, 67

Quotations from *The Last Romantic* found on pages: 27, 67

Quotations from *In Search of True Wisdom* found on page 141

Quotations from "The Consolation of my Grief" found on page 150

Quotations from "My Mama" found on pages: 154, 183

Quotations from *Life Transfigured* found on page 167

Quotations from nun's interviews found on pages 153, 154

Quotations from *Bran Castle* found on pages: 61, 62, 67, 75, 76